S0-CRE-405

Introduction

Operations is at the core of service delivery and meeting Customer demands. With such high visibility, it is often the first function startup companies must execute well. As a company grows, however, management attention must focus on nonoperational areas, such as sales growth and finance, for good reason.

My experiences have shown me that in many fast-growing companies, the focus often remains on sales, development and finance and does not always return to operations. To continue being successful companies must consciously focus on customer-oriented operations. As a company grows rapidly, a failure to keep operations top of mind can sometimes can leave existing Customers behind.

Excellence in operations, particularly in repeatable processes, can seem mundane to visionary leaders of private-equity or venture capital-backed firms. And although strong leaders may not dream of processes in the middle of the night, they do know it is critical for the success and continuous improvement of their companies and that they need to find captains who thrive in that area.

As a result, companies that have excellence in operations are more innovative, more responsive to Customers and clients, and more able to rapidly adapt to market trends. With the additional capacity that operations excellence provides, companies are more likely to achieve their visions since they have costs under control and can see around corners.

So, what is the purpose of *The Power of Lean Process*?

While it does lower costs, reduce waste, increase team member morale and address Customer needs, the business benefits of a Lean approach are more strategic than that. Among other strategic areas, *The Power of Lean Process* addresses four questions:

1. Is a company's ability and operational capacity able to keep pace with the growth of sales, particularly in entrepreneurial, high growth companies?
2. Does a company have a systemic repository of IP and an effective way to train team members?
3. Does the leadership team have confidence in its organization to manage Customer-facing defects without getting personally involved in each issue?
4. Does the leadership team have the capacity to focus on strategic areas without feeling like they are getting disproportionally pulled into company operations?

These strategic considerations associated with *The Power of Lean Process* add a 20,000-foot perspective and emphasize that an organization's achievement of strategic objectives is an ongoing journey. With an operations capacity that delights Customers, has cost predictability, and has the confidence of the executive leadership team, a firm has a much higher ability and freedom to focus on its visions and its dreams. This is the power of lean process.

Many conference speakers and webinars have discussed robotic process automation and artificial intelligence for business leaders. The presenters often seem to compete against each other for command of minute technical details of data cleansing, data concepts, and the nuances of big data. The business leaders leave confused, thinking, "How can artificial intelligence help my business, and how do I get started?" Tomorrow's economy will almost certainly include the widespread application of robotic process automation. Having solid processes will be a prerequisite in the same manner that today's physical robot putting a windshield on a car needs a human — who has done it manually — to tell the robot what to do. This book intends to bring clarity to how repeatable processes can benefit businesses, including in the preparation of a world of robotic process automation and artificial intelligence. There are scores of technical books discussing the technical elements of Lean and Six Sigma. If a Six Sigma black belt is looking for a better formula to lower a control limit or execute a Monte Carlo simulation, this isn't that book. This book is for business practitioners looking to put continuous improvement to work, and preparing for tomorrow's economy

The Power of Lean Process will give you strategies to leverage operations excellence so you can achieve your company's dreams. Because Lean is such a structured approach, it is different from other business improvement concepts, many of which rely solely on team member motivation or deep theoretical thinking. I believe the Lean-related tools and processes conveyed in these pages can significantly transform the health of your company in 12 months.

Chapter 2

Setting Company Key Imperatives

"When you set out to take Vienna, take Vienna."
— *Napoleon Bonaparte*

It is important to clearly articulate a company's key expectations. In the classic book *First Break All the Rules*, Marcus Buckingham lists some fundamental questions companies should ask team members to assess engagement. One question is, "Do you know what is expected of you when you show up at work?"

A critical part of optimizing a company's operations is to have clear, company-wide goals and imperatives. This facilitates the alignment of the organization from top to bottom, and allows leadership imperatives to cascade down throughout the organization. In his many essays, Jack Welch, the former CEO of General Electric, consistently stressed the importance of having clear business imperatives. In his memoir, *Winning*, he says that while at GE, he made sure that the company's core mission and values were repeated in various forms around the organization so frequently that team members could probably recite them in their sleep. Welch tells a fable in which he wakes up one of his team members from a deep slumber and asks him to repeat a GE division's core mission and values — and the team member does it, albeit with a little bit of trouble due to her sleepy-eyed stupor. The directional clarity this represents allows organizations to be aligned across the hierarchy, despite a wide variety of functions, perspectives and experiences.

In a company I ran, we posted our quarterly Key Imperatives for all team members to see. Additionally, we also posted retired Key Imperatives on the wall to proudly document several years' history of continuous improvement.

A lack of clear, understandable and pervasive imperatives can cause many issues. In David Allen's *Getting Things Done*, the author states that the No. 1 source of stress among team members is constantly dealing with preventable work crises. He further explains that these crises are usually due to leaders failing to make important decisions within an appropriate timeframe. Mangers that take too long to make decisions exacerbates and intensifies frequent crisis situations, but it is typically not the root cause.

Team cannot blame all crisis situations on simple human error — many issues run much deeper than that in that they create a chaotic environment that is ripe for error. What is the root cause of the all-to-frequent business crises that lead to team member stress? It depends on the organization, but a good place to start looking for underlying breakdown areas is within five common pitfalls of strategic planning. These five pitfalls emphasize the importance of having clear, company-wide imperatives for team members to follow:

The Five Pitfalls of Strategic Planning

1. *Unaligned Leadership*

This pitfall is when members of leadership as well as other members of the organization don't share the same priorities or goals, that is, company-wide key imperatives. One executive sees one version of the organization's priorities based on their viewpoint, while another executive sees completely different set of goals. With different sets of priorities, each leader may be in conflict with the other. When this is the case, numerous issues can arise and cause confusion in the middle and lower levels of the organization. The Chinese general, military strategist and philosopher General Sun Tzu said, "If words of command are not clear and distinct, if orders are not thoroughly understood, then the general is to blame." The eighteenth president of the United States, General Ulysses S. Grant, was also known for his clarity of orders.

2. Changing Priorities

How many of us have scars from being in organizations with changing priorities, whether set by leaders chasing shiny objects or failing to see thought-critical projects to the end? A crisis can easily arise when management changes its mind about which projects are important in the middle of working on the first set of priorities. This can waste a considerable amount of time, resources and emotional energy, and can end up causing wasteful rework. Having key imperatives for management and other team members while also having the discipline to stick with them can mitigate this risk.

3. Unrealistic Scope

This is an easy pitfall to which we fall victim. We are always told to reach for the stars and boldly strike out toward the best possible outcome in all areas of life. We're told that fortune favors the bold, and that action is better than non-action. And a lot of the time, all of that advice is useful and mostly true. But sometimes, being too bold and having grandiose expectations can be risky.

For several years, I was on the board of directors at the Cheer Guild of Riley Hospital for Children, an organization that provided comfort such as toys, games, and art and music therapy to children in the hospital. My role was focused on strategy process, and I used to always refer to a specific analogy when managing our strategy. Think of a house. It's a standard house, with a foundation, a main floor for living, an attic and a roof. There is nothing special about this house. But it represents how we should prioritize strategy in business.

ARRANGE PRIORITIES LIKE A HOUSE: FOUNDATION, MAIN FLOOR, AND THEN ATTIC

The foundation of a house is its most important part. Without the foundation, the house may stand up and act as a functional living space for a while, but it will eventually succumb to its instability and collapse in a pile of brick and wood, and in the process, utterly fail its residents.

In the business world, this foundation is the management of risk. Before anything else can be sought, before any other projects can begin, initiatives that may cause risk to the organization must be dealt with, such as accounting, regulatory issues, or strategic alignment with investors or banks.

This may seem counter to what we are told growing up, and are often told in the business world. I have always liked to favor bold behavior — it's the American way, after all. In fact, most entrepreneurs are risk-takers by nature; it's practically a required trait in the trade. While we're on the rare topic of risk mitigation rather than risk extension, consider an anecdote.

One particular game of golf with my father-in-law illustrated the problem of risk to me quite well. He was, and still is these years later, somewhat of an expert golf player. He wasn't a PGA pro, but he played multiple rounds every week, so he certainly knew his way around the game.

I, on the other hand, only have time to play one or two rounds every year, so I was at a disadvantage in terms of experience. As we played, my father-in-law gave me tips and pointers and talked to me about general golf strategy.

At one point in the game, as you always do at some point, we came to a water hazard — a medium-sized pond — and I was faced with two choices concerning risk: be bold and go for it, hitting the ball all the way over the pond from my current position; or play it safe and lay up closer to the water's edge so that I would have a much better chance to clear the pond on my next shot.

My father-in-law recommended that I go for the latter option and simply layup. He told me that golf is more often than not a game about reducing your risk and not going for it, contrary to popular thought. This was at first difficult for me to swallow and seemed an almost counterintuitive way to play. But I thought about how behind I would be if I did hit my ball in the water and decided to follow his advice. I cleared the pond in two shots without an issue.

This golfing experience was somewhat of a paradigm shift for me, and it made me see that while simply going for it is a good strategy sometimes, it is key to know when to play it safe and secure the goal.

He was full of these kinds of risk-averse pieces of advice, such as never having any less than a half tank of gas in your car. This might seem excessive, but by following this advice, you reduce your chances of running out of gas to, effectively, zero percent. Running out of gas is an unlikely thing under any circumstances, but if it does happen, it can be a massive hassle. Avoiding it at a small cost, therefore, makes a lot of sense.

But back to the house construction analogy. Once all risk is managed and mitigated as best as it can be, the next step, the main floor of the house, can be built. This main floor is where the house's tenants do the bulk of their living. Most of the "living" for a business is in improving operations. This is the kind of stuff Lean production optimizes.

Finally, there is the attic. Once you have optimized operations, at least for the time being, innovation and growth can be addressed. In the case of my service on the hospital board, these areas included our hospital's role in expanding programs to Kenya and other projects designed to extend influence and innovation. These future-focused initiatives will vary for your organization. The important part is to start with understanding and reining in risk so you can get to place where working on your vision and future makes sense. One of the advantage of stable processes is to allow decision makers to add risk to their profile in a conscious, innovation manner – the attic activities. Extending the company portfolio into riskier activities (like innovation) while maintaining an unnecessarily high level of risk in basic operations can put your company at a risk level it does not to be in. De-risk your main floor through process so you can add risk to your innovation and growth initiatives.

4. Unclear Processes

This is an obvious pitfall, to be sure. A large portion of this book addresses this issue, so I won't go into detail here. Simplify and optimize the process at the manual level before automating it and making it flashy and fast.

5. Lack of Project Management

This is the final pitfall that can lead to crises and stress. Project management is another topic that will be covered in great detail later on in this book — stay tuned.

Part Three

Visualizing Your Processes

Chapter 3

The Five S's

"When we really delve into the reasons for why we can't let something go, there are only two: an attachment to the past or a fear for the future."
— *Marie Kondo, #1 New York Times best-selling author of* Spark Joy *and* The Life-Changing Magic of Tidying Up

An easily overlooked but essential step to becoming a Lean organization is the implementation and continual following of the Five S's. These are five words that begin with "S" and refer to improvement activities aimed at increasing the cleanliness, orderliness and general organization of a work area for greater efficiency and the reduction of waste. The Five S's are actually five Japanese words beginning with S, translated to English S words.

The first three S's are tactical, and the last two are strategic.

The Five S's

1. **Sort**
2. **Set in order / Straighten**
3. **Sanitize / Shine**
4. **Standardize**
5. **Sustain**

In addition to striving for general efficiency and an overall waste reduction, the high-level goals of the Five S's align quite well with the goals of a Lean organization in general.

The goals of the Five S's are to:

- Make money.
- Reduce waste.
- Increase speed.
- Make each person's job easier.
- Help each person become a successful manager of their workplace.
- Improve the success of the workplace.
- Support a culture of pride and excellence.

Note, I started with "make money." To the untrained manager, the Five S's may be more about having a tidy workspace or addressing obsessive compulsive disorder impulses. I had a quality manager who had a sign on her desk reading, "I'm not OCD, I'm CDO, because that's in alphabetical order."

Whether your assets are hand tools, office supplies, kitchen utensils or computer files, having just the right amount of inventory and being able to access your gear or information fast is a competitive advantage for any business, one that can make or save you money.

Think about the relationship between order and speed. Imagine a frustrated Customer is on the phone and you need to address their issue with data. A mechanic is being called on to bring critical uptime for a water system. Or someone needs to address an IRS audit and find scanned documents on a hard drive. Does it matter if people are fast or slow in these scenarios? You bet it is better to be fast. The Five S's create operational excellence to support such speed.

In today's data-rich world, often we are as at risk of having too much data than too little. Between five of us with digital cameras in cell phones, my family takes between 5,000 and 10,000 digital photos a year. I don't have the personal capacity to make a scrapbook of the photos like my mom did—there's way too much content. So, we save the best two to three photos for our holiday card and I download the rest of the photos to a hard drive. I tell myself I'll organize them someday…

BENEFITS OF THE FIVE S'S

As the above graphic illustrates, the Five S's improve many aspects of an organization and eliminate numerous kinds of waste. Like aspects of the quality movement, Five S's were originally invented to address systems in factories, rather than service industries. Disorder in factories may have focused around tools and machinery, but common kinds of disorder addressed by the Five S's can be applied to service companies in ways such as the following:

- The organization of floor space.
- Bulletin and communication boards.
- Document control and storage.
- File organization.
- Office and maintenance supplies.

On the surface the Five S's are somewhat general and can be interpreted in many ways depending on the situation or context. In the context of Lean, however, they refer specifically to the following processes.

1. ***Sort (tactical)***

   The first step to utilizing the Five S's is to Sort, or identify the waste. This can be applied to any situation in which there is waste that needs to be eliminated, but office and work space organization is a common one.

   In this example, one method may be to visually tag items in the work area as either red, yellow or green items. Red items are definitely not needed, yellow items may be needed on occasion, and green items are needed frequently.

   Another example that can put this in perspective occurred on the old television show *Clean Sweep*. The premise of the show was that the hosts and their crew would go into people's houses, which were always notably dirty or disorganized, and help the residents clean and organize them.

   In one episode, the hosts were helping a man who, for a variety of reasons, had 50 pairs of khaki pants stuffed in his closet. This was seen as wasteful and not a good start to living a more organized life, so the hosts and their team devised a plan to get rid of most of the man's khaki pants.

   First, they divided the pants on the man's front lawn into three sections using colored rope. The man was to place each pair of khakis into one of the three sections: the left section was where he was to place the pants he definitely wanted to keep, the middle section was for pants he was unsure of, and the right section was for pants he could certainly get rid of. This last pile went to a charity such as Goodwill. Eventually, the man had placed all of his pairs of khakis into the three sections on the lawn. This process was akin to the Sort process of the Five S's.

2. Set in Order / Straighten (tactical)

After sorting possible wasteful items or activities, the next step is to set them into order, or straighten them. There is a place for everything, and everything should be kept in its place. This is the goal of the second S. Putting everything in its right place.

In an office space, this step might involve organizing the items marked as yellow and green even further, prioritizing each individual item to be stored in a location in the office based on how frequently it is used, similar to how you might sort your closet — in the summer, summer clothes should be the most easily accessed, while heavy winter clothing should be packed in the back of the closet, out of the way of all the summer clothes.

Let's return to *Clean Sweep* for a moment. In the Sort stage, the man sorted all of his pairs of pants into three sections: keep, not sure and don't keep. He ended up placing the majority of the pants in the middle "not sure" section. This is the section the show's team focused on Setting in Order. They asked him about why he put so many pairs of pants in the middle section, and he would always have a reason for keeping the pants. For example, he said that he wanted to keep one pair of pants because they were the pants he got engaged in.

The team took this information and talked around it, eventually convincing him to move almost all of the pants into the right section to be removed forever, leaving six pairs of khakis in the left section to be kept. This is the Set in Order / Straighten step of the Five S's. All of those pairs of pants had a place — the team simply needed to put them where they belonged.

3. Sanitize and Shine (tactical)

After sorting and setting in order, the next step is to make things clean and good-looking. Dirt and disorder are defects, and the goal of this step is to eliminate them. In the office organization example, this would mean a thorough cleaning of the entire work area. What happens when you clean everything off your desk and you remove that big monitor from the back of your desk? Dust bunnies, crumbs and coffee stains can often be found and cleaned—this is the sanitize and shine part.

This may seem a less critical step, but a clean work area is much easier to keep organized, and in turn is a much more productive environment, and also instills a sense of pride and ownership in the area.

In *Clean Sweep*, while one team was helping the man sort and straighten his massive collection of khakis, another team was Sanitizing and Shining his closet. They removed all of his old hangers and replaced them with six beautiful mahogany pants hangers. When the man brought the six remaining pairs of pants inside to hang them in his closet, he was thrilled to see the beautiful hangers for his pants, and hung them up as neatly as he could. His closet had been Sanitized and Shined. He would now be more motivated to keep it clean and organized. However, *Clean Sweep* ends here. The show couldn't afford to constantly check up on the man to make sure he was following the final two of the Five S's.

4. Standardize (strategic)

The final two S's of the five refer back to the organization and implementation of the first three, which is why they are considered strategic. After sorting, straightening and sanitizing a work space, the next step is to Standardize the sorting, straightening and sanitizing process. Establish a common methodology for carrying out the first three steps of the five.

Do this by establishing consistent, exact tasks assigned in a standard way to the individuals in the work space, and create checklists for these tasks to ensure they are carried out. Basically, this step is to establish and write an operating procedure (OP) for the first three S's.

Even though our *Clean Sweep* example came to an end prematurely, we can continue in a similar vein. When I was a child, my sister and I always got new clothes for school every summer and Christmas. My mother, to ensure that we wouldn't collect too many items of clothing to properly store, implemented a standardization process. Each time we bought new clothes for the coming school year (my favorites were always Sears Toughskins), we had to take out all of the clothes in our closets and dressers and decide whether each of our clothing items was worth keeping, and then take the ones not worth keeping down the street to donate them to families in need of clothes. This is similar to a standardization process. We maintained the cleanliness and organization of our closets through the procedure established by my mom.

5. Sustain

After establishing a standard process for keeping the work space clean and orderly, Sustaining that process is the final step. The culture of the organization must be changed in order to ensure that the gains you've experienced via the Five S's process are continued into the future.

The first step to this is to measure your progress against your original baseline condition. For example, take a look at the items tagged green, yellow and red, and consider how well you're sustaining this sort of sorting and setting in order. How well are keeping your space clean and orderly? What are the improvements you've experienced since these changes were made? Continue to measure your progress under the Five S's, and create case studies and checklists for each of the S's to be disseminated. Next, you need a project plan that details the rollout of the Five S's across your entire team, division, organization, etc.

Finally, once all this is completed, don't forget to set up a system to reward accomplishments under the Five S's for your team members. If we look back to my childhood clothes shopping, my mom's method of sustaining our standardized, organized closets was to ensure that our process of purging unwanted clothes to allow room for the new was repeated twice a year — at Christmas and just before school began in the summer.

I'm sure she did not roll out a project plan regarding this process — perhaps she would have shared it with my father — but in any event, she stuck to this process for many years, until my sister and I were old enough to take care of our own closet organization process. Here are some key attributes related to the fifth S, which is often the most difficult of the Five to successfully implement or follow:

- Education
- Training
- Continuous improvement
- Inspection
- Feedback
- Total team member involvement
- Peer-to-peer coaching
- Discipline

As I mentioned, there are many ways to apply and integrate this set of steps and their philosophies into your organization, but probably the most common way is in work space organization. Another is in file organization, which is a subset of workplace organization but warrants deeper discussion because it is extremely important.

REAL WORLD: Disorganized data deemed useless

A few years back, I was in charge of processes and methods for the Brussels office of a technology company. One day, the COO approached me and told me that we were growing, and would be closing down the Brussels office to open three new offices: one in London, one in Frankfurt and one in Paris.

During the transition process, I discovered that there were five whole years' worth of unorganized files on the Brussels servers. I notified upper management about this issue, and when they asked me how long it would take to organize the files enough to transfer them and make them useful again, I gave them the hard truth: the files were all organized in such a haphazard fashion that it would take a two-person team six months to Five-S. This was too much money, and so instead, they took the server hard drives and placed them in a safety deposit box, never to be looked at again. All that data was useless to us because it was so poorly organized.

This would not have been the case had we implemented the Five S's system at any point before the very end. We could have benefited from five years' worth of intellectual property.

There is always a price to be paid for disorganization. While the urgency of the next project loudly begs for attention it is still important to leave digital and physical files in a coherent structure. But our work space (our servers and hard drives) remained unkempt, and we paid for it in the end.

That situation is exactly the kind of thing the Five S's aim to mitigate and avoid altogether. Use the disciplined approach of the Five S's to organize, and in doing so, optimize, your work place and organization as a whole.

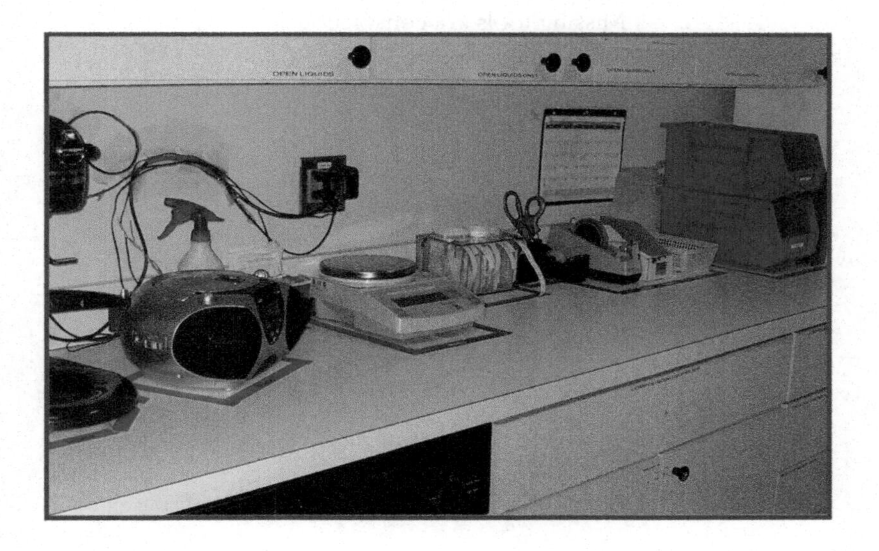

A pharmacy workstation, using labeled blue tape to outline each fixture. At the end of each workday, each item was put back in its place.

Tools are put away in their outlined areas.
Missing tools are conspicuous.

Chapter 4

The Level I Value Stream Map and Triaging Modules

"A good process produces good results. Focus on the process of what it takes to be successful."

— *Nick Saban, University of Alabama football coach*

We have seen an example of a small, continuous improvement initiative. Let's take the perspective up a level and look at the processes of a company from a 20,000-foot view. The first phase of a company beginning a comprehensive initiative in Lean Sigma is to create a Level I Process Map.

A central value of the Level I Process Map is the visualization of a process. In the same way a graph allows the user to visualize a table of data, process maps bring systems to life. I love the title of the value stream mapping book *Learning to See* by Mike Rother and John Shook. It captures the essence of the value of the map: visualization of the process, which is a catalyst for transparency, alignment and communication.

In a complex organization, it can take 10-100 hours of support operations to make possible one hour of core operations. For example, in the military, imagine the effort it takes to facilitate a fighter jet's one-hour flight in battle. Think of the food, medicine, fuel, spare parts, communications, security, training, planning, air traffic control, accounting and countless other functions that must be performed for the fighter jet to complete its critical mission – which may take less than an hour. Similarly in medicine, for a 10-minute physician appointment to treat a sore throat, there exist numerous hours of support from I marketing, scheduling, vital sign collection, lab testing, insurance billing, facilities management, payroll and scores of other business functions required to support that visit. The Level I Process Map allows you to more clearly see these relationships.

The Level I Process Map is a mutually exclusive, collectively exhaustive (or MECE, pronounced "mee-see") visual management diagram of the entire company. Ideally it is one page, perhaps two.

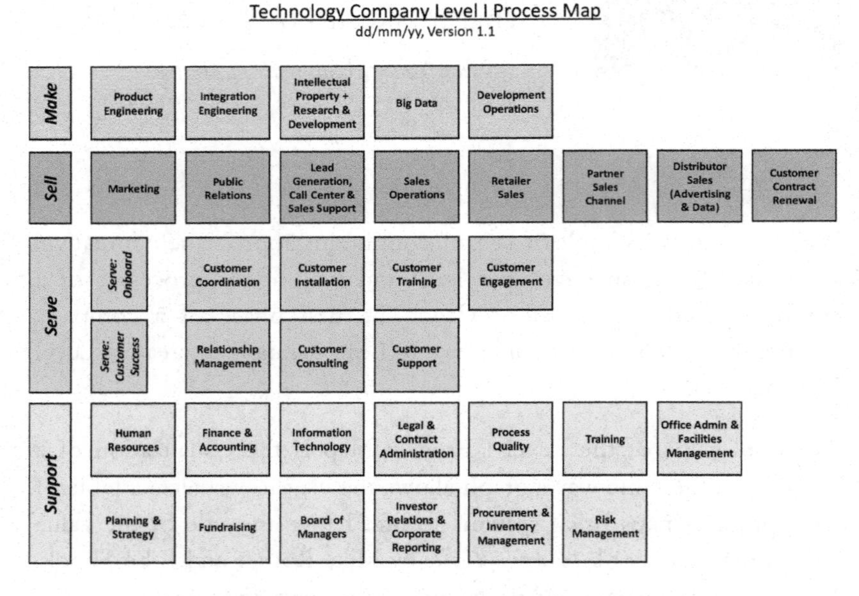

AN EXAMPLE OF A LEVEL I PROCESS MAP

One of my favorite podcasts is called Manager Tools. The hosts say that their guidance is for 90 percent of the people 90 percent of the time. That framework applies to the guidelines and suggestions in this book. Almost by definition, there will certainly be times when your Lean journey won't address every exception.

Recently, the pilot Sully Sullenberger was interviewed about a plane crash, now that he is the world-renown expert after successfully landing his plane in the Hudson River. He was asked about the potential causes of the crash early in the investigation. He said that "as aviation safety has become better, as aviation accidents have become more rare, their causes have actually become more unique, and because aviation has done such as good job of reducing and eliminating what used to be many common causes of accidents, what we are left with are more 'black swan' events."

This is relevant in our discussion, as it is the Lean practitioner's role to continually lower the water level in the stream, exposing the lower rocks to confront in order to get to smooth waters. This is a common analogy where the waters look smooth on the surface, but when the water level is lowered, some rocks appear. You remove those rocks, they lower the water again. It is similar to when Eliyahu Goldratt, in *The Goal*, says that when you open a bottleneck in an operations system, another, less severe bottleneck always appears.

A Level I Process Map

Let's examine the steps to developing a Level I Process Map.

Prelude to Step 1: Process Map Basics

First, a note on formatting, one that applies to all documentation. Good formatting creates readability, which creates focus, which creates persuasion.

I spend a fair amount of time on making sure documents are tightly formatted. Anyone who has had to suffer through poorly structured PowerPoints, Excel documents printed in an illogical manner, or Word documents with no page numbers or dates can relate to the waste managers deal with as they review documents. These documents may have the potential to persuade prospects, leaders and team members, so why would an author who spent time and treasure to create documents with great content fail to address distracting formatting?

Always include a date and version number, on both printouts and file names. Any experienced project manager has suffered through a lack of version control, causing rework, confusion and delay, yet I see these basic controls lacking in virtually every company I consult. Good Lean practitioners implementing continuous improvement will have many versions of documents. Use discipline, and always date and version-number each document.

When I receive a spreadsheet, particularly a complex one, I start by formatting it. I maximize the margins, add a footer with date, page numbers and the filename; I default to fitting the spreadsheet onto one page, and if that is too small, expand from there. It's like when you sit down to read a new book, creasing the spine, fanning the pages, examining the table of contents, getting a feel for the length of the chapters, seeing if there is an insert of photos and forming a plan in your mind to attack the book. Allow your audience a similar experience with the format of your Level I Process Map, and the reader will digest and accept it more readily.

When I was a consultant at Accenture, I was trained to proofread formatting in a PowerPoint slide deck by isolating one formatting area, such as the font, size and placement of a slide title, and reviewing every page in the deck for that area only. Then I'd go to the front of the deck and proofread each slide for the next area, such as the formatting of bullet points. Their position was that it is easy to lose track of formatting discipline when trying to analyze each slide for multiple items.

Step 2: Guidelines for Good Structure

As you can see in the sample Level I Process Map that appears earlier in this chapter, the rows of categories progress according to specific function areas. I have no strict rules for developing the Level I Process Map, but I do have a few guidelines. The guidelines correlate with the high-level structure of most organizations, e.g., product development, sales, operations and corporate center, following the order of business: make it, sell it, support it.

1. **Make:** The first row should be product development for companies such as manufacturing and software companies.
2. **Sell:** Make the next row sales and business development modules.

3. **Serve:** The next two or three rows are for the core operations modules of the company. Consider sub categories of client onboarding, Customer success and other "steady state" operations for service companies.
4. **Support:** The last row or two are corporate center operations modules, such as human resources and finance.
5. As with all documents, always include a title, header or footer, date, version number and owner.

Step 3: The Interview

The best way to start a Level I Process Map is with sharpies, sticky notes and a large wall, or flipchart paper on a table. There are a few roles in this work session: one facilitator and at least one Subject Matter Experts (SME). The facilitator organizes sticky notes, captures content electronically after the exercise, formats it and reformats it. The SMEs just focus on content. They are like the diners in a restaurant; the facilitator is the waiter. Ideally, the SMEs are not thinking about the logistics and Lean stuff; they are thinking about the just processes in which they are experts. Diners in a restaurant want to enjoy each other's company, delegating all the service details to the waiter. The Lean facilitator should assume those duties.

In the exercise, the facilitator, prepped with a set of colored, oversized sticky notes and colored, markers, interviews the SMEs, asking questions such as:

- "What do we do here at our company?"
- "What are the high-level business processes that we execute?"
- "Which team is tasked with each high-level business process?"
- "Are all team members represented on these sticky notes? Who is missing and under which process do they fall?"

The facilitator will write each process on a post-it note and put it on the wall, taking periodic breaks to organize and sort the notes in some logical order.

This is similar to a brainstorming session where participants go for quantity, not quality, and should not be evaluated or deterred by others judging them for the right answer. Let the facilitator sort and organize.

Step 4: Process Map Evaluation and Improvement

Generally, publishing the Level I Process Map and letting the SMEs review it for clarity, accuracy and comprehensiveness over a period of a few days will result in adjustments. They should also make sure it is MECE (mutually exclusive, collectively exhaustive). Don't be frustrated with changes – iterating the Level I Process Map is expected and a sign of progress in the development of the content. I have iterated on process maps 10-20 times in the first phase of an intensive process-mapping session, and up to 50 times over the course of five years. Always use discipline in iterating the 10th of the version number (e.g., 1.0 to 1.1) when distributing any documentation. As discussed, version control is critical in reducing confusion and waste. I've been in many meetings where we return from the printer and distribute the new version and collect the old versions to maintain version control and to keep people from being confused by looking or editing a prior version.

Step 5: Process Prioritization

Once the Level I Process Map is created, the next step is to prioritize it. I suggest you triage your modules (the boxes of your process map), grouping them into three priority categories: high, medium and low priority. If you are implementing a Lean quality system in an existing business, as opposed to a startup, you'll probably have a feel for which modules need to be addressed first. It is likely that one or more of these criteria, such as getting pressure from Customers for defects, were the cause of initiating a Lean program in the first place. Note you are not prioritizing the value of the business module, but rather, the need for that business module to receive Lean and continuous improvement attention, a process we called "working it." If a module has been "worked," we have recently analyzed that system and taken waste out of it.

The following are five sample criteria you can use to prioritize your business modules:

1. ***Processes causing Customer-facing defects*** that have affected quality in the eyes of the Customer. It may be critical that you address these early in the process.
2. ***Core business processes*** that are fundamental to your operations. Examples might be managing narcotics for a pharmacy, running payroll for an HR company or food preparation in a restaurant.
3. ***Strategic processes*** that could drive the future success of your company, such as research and development, marketing, or a product or service offering you expect to drive your company's success.
4. ***Cash flow-driving processes*** that can impact your cash, such as inventory levels, accounts receivable or accounts payable.
5. ***Processes related to low morale and team member turnover*** that frustrate your team members or cause them to rethink their viability as members of your firm.

Given that criteria, various methods exist for prioritizing modules. I've included two for you to consider.

Method One: Team Members assign high, medium or low to each module.

Note their grade is not about answering the question, "How important is this business function?" but rather, "What is the importance of the Lean Sigma team working on this module for continuous improvement?" Thus, a very important business function such as sales may be low in continuous improvement priority because it is running smoothly, has recently been "worked" or has already been addressed by a Lean team.

This exercise for prioritizing modules is to have a team of experts — the people who do the work — assign each module a high, medium or low score.

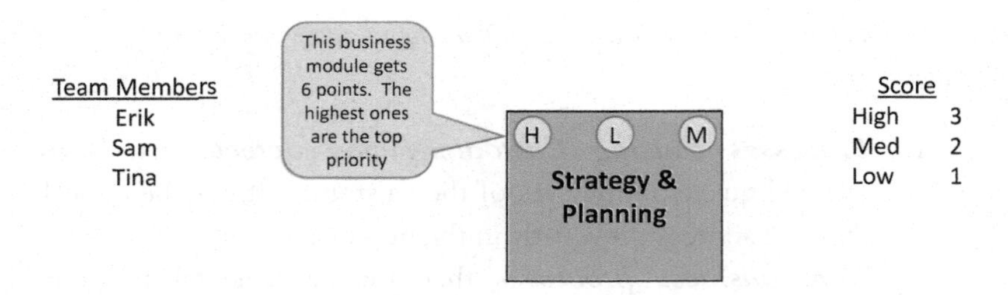

This first method is a bit time consuming because there is an exhaustive survey of every business module. But at the end of the analysis, it generates a quick, thorough diagnosis for every business function. This can be particularly helpful if a team is doing the analysis and the results are presented to the CEO, executive leadership team or board of directors for a bird's-eye view of the Lean status of the company.

Method Two: Team members identify their top five business modules to work on.

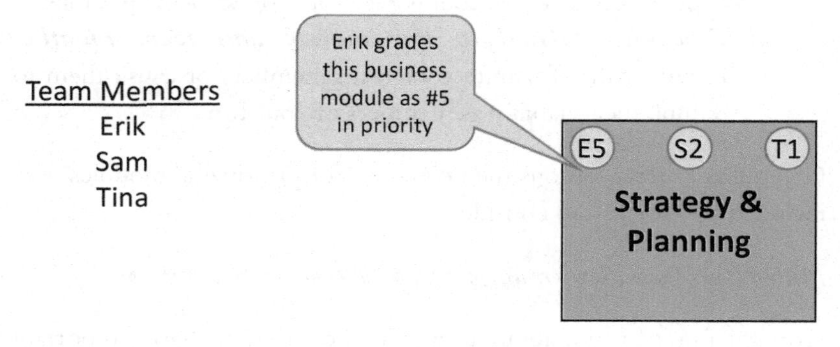

This second method creates a "heat map" of the top priority business modules — an at-a-glance view of what needs to be worked. It also shows the specific perspectives of each manager, and understanding the perspectives of different functions might be insightful. The modules' prioritization can either be numbers of dots or a score of the module, as in Method One.

At this point in the Lean journey, you are armed with a Level I Process Map and clear priorities. In the next chapter, you will learn how to use these tools to create Level II Process Maps of the highest priority business modules.

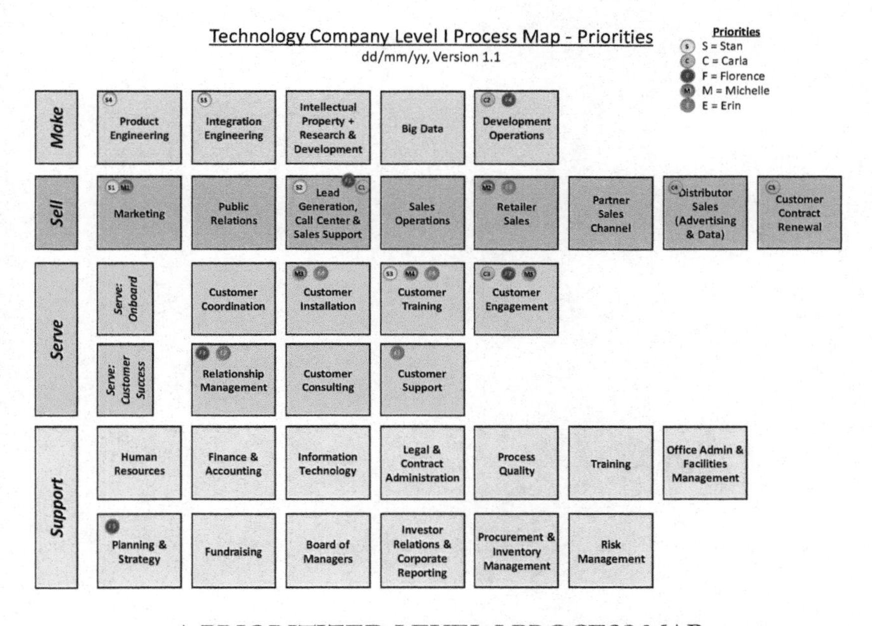

A PRIORITIZED LEVEL I PROCESS MAP

Part Four

Creating Repeatable, Defect-Free Processes

Chapter 5

The Level II Value Stream Map: Documenting a Business System

"It takes time to create excellence. If it could be done quickly, more people would do it."

— John Wooden, former UCLA basketball coach and winner of 10 NCAA championships

With our level I Process Map prepared and triaged, it's time to begin the Level II Process Map. This is a detailed process map of one of the 20-50 business modules in the Level I map.

The Level II map is more technical and detail oriented than the Level I map. It will likely require considerable input from subject matter experts (SMEs).

A Process Map Is Like a Sculpture

Creating this map is like sculpting. If you imagine a statue of a woman in the stages of its creation, it starts out as a block of marble. After a period of time, you can see a head emerge. And then general features begin to form. You can tell that the statue is a woman, as you can distinguish her face, neck and shoulders. After more time, you can make out rough details and facial features. Finally, you can see all the fine elements of the figure — the hair, eyes, expression. This is what the creation of a detailed Level II Process Map is like.

It requires a rough process flow, and then the map gets more and more detailed with finer points delineated. To create a good map, perhaps like a good statue, a Lean practitioner will work it over and over with SMEs. It can be tedious, repetitious and laborious. It takes patience.

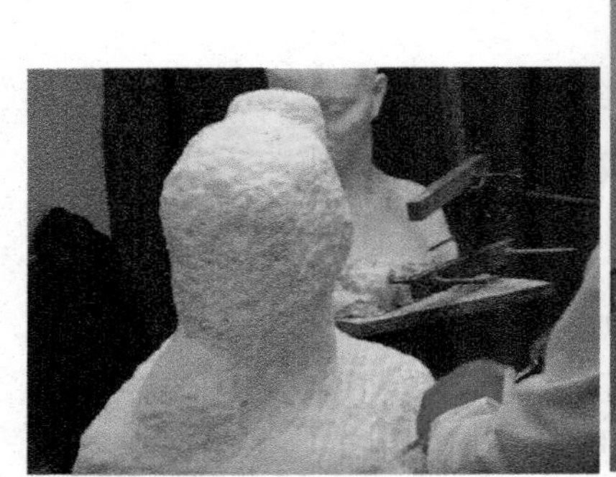

CREATING A PROCESS MAP IS LIKE SCULPTING.

The process should start by documenting the *current condition.* As noted earlier, this is the way things are now, warts and all. There can be a parking lot list of items that the organization might want to improve in the future in order to create the target condition. This status will require a series of rapid improvement events to accomplish the goal.

Process Maps Are a Form of Visual Management

Visual management is a critical Lean concept. As we are discussing process maps, let's explore the wider concept of visual management. Visual management is an enabler of communication. In the same way a graph communicates data so much more clearly and faster than a table of data, process maps bring to life information that may be contained in another format, such as an operating procedure (OP).

Process Map Attributes

There are several attributes that I recommend when creating a process map.

1. Flow steps from left to right. Don't double back, even if it saves white space. If you must double back have two broad rows with only one doubling-back of flow
2. Have either a main flow on the top row from left-to-right, and have sub-processes in the corresponding columns under the main row; or a main flow on the left column top-to-bottom and have sub-processes in rows from left to right.
3. Minimize the crossing of flow lines. This can be an art.
4. As in all documents, always include a date version number, and owner.
5. Use color coding to indicate the completeness of the underlying OP, such as green for complete, yellow for in-process, and red for not-started.

There Are Limitless Process Map Formats

After researching process maps, one will find there are scores of formats. The following are some formats I've seen successfully — and unsuccessfully — utilized. Pick your poison.

PROCESS MAP WITH SWIM LANES

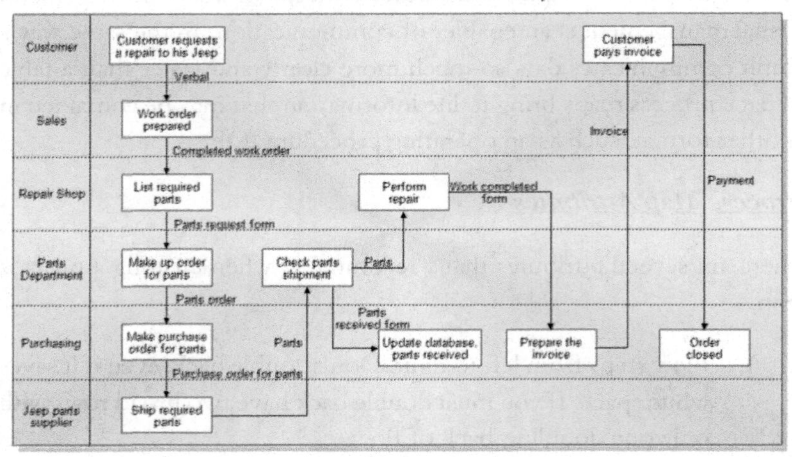

Using swim lanes in a process map indicates each owner of a process. If multiple people or entities participate in a process, each has a lane. For example, in ordering a hamburger and a drink in a McDonald's drive through, there would be a swim lane for the Customer, the team member taking the order, the cashier, the person making the burger, and perhaps the person filling the drink.

The advantage is that swim lanes make the participants in a process visible. The disadvantage is that swim lanes typically create a lot of white space, assuming there is chronological flow from left to right.

PROCESS MAP WITH MULTI-DIRECTIONAL FLOW

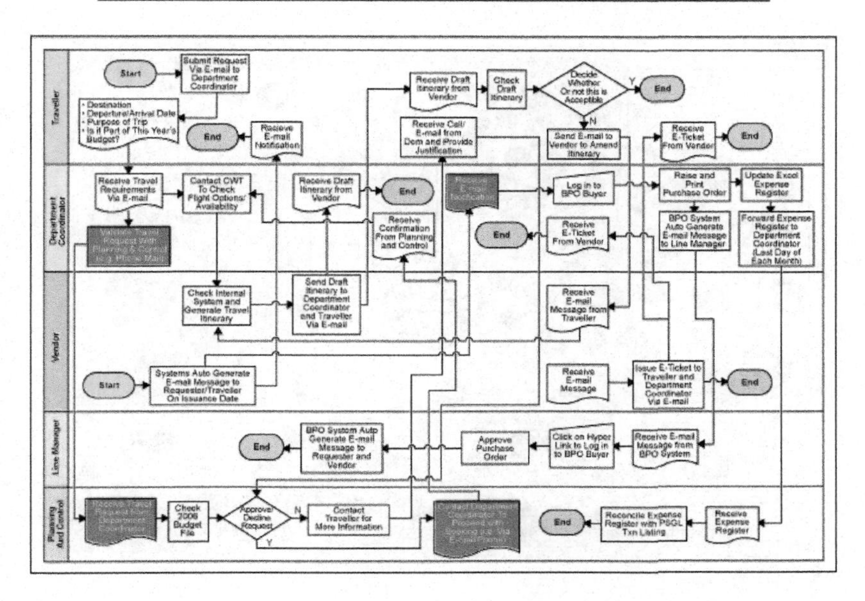

This is an example of a confusing process map, a violation of the guideline of left-to-right flow. I find this to be defeating the purpose of a process map — to add clarity, visibility and insight to a process through visual management.

A PROCESS MAP DESIGNED TO COVEY CHAOS

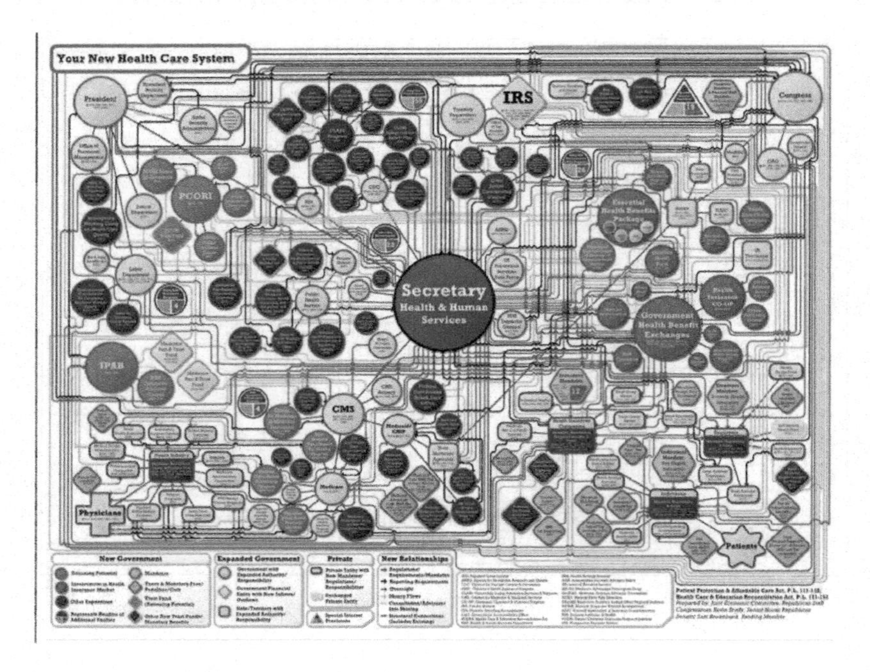

If you're trying to prove a point regarding the utter failure of a process, this example illustrates how effective a process map can be.

CHARLES MINARD'S MAP OF NAPOLEON'S RUSSIAN CAMPAIGN IN 1812

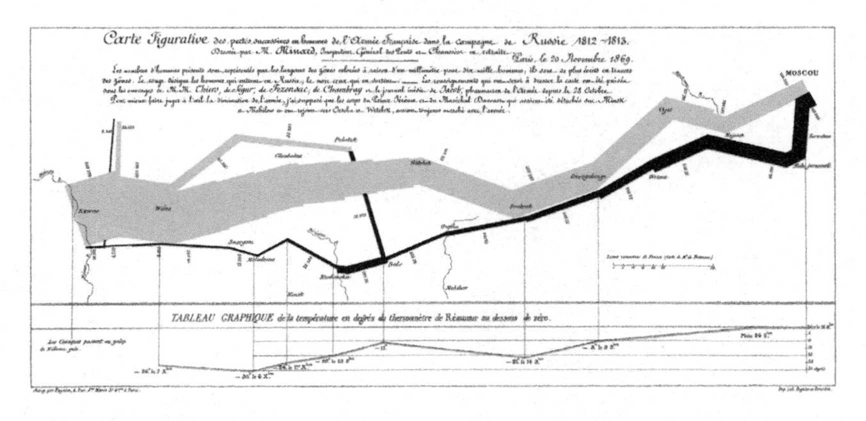

This is what is often cited as one of the best visual management maps in history. Minard, a French engineer and statistician, shows Napoleon's unsuccessful invasion of Russia in 1812. Napoleon invades Russia in June with over 400,000 troops. Russia's strategy is a scorched earth plan, burning all farms, houses and resources in an effort to slow the French advance as winter approaches. The lack of food and shelter, along with a brutal winter, forces the invaders to retreat.

The area is a map, with Prussia on the left and Russia on the right. The top brown line shows the advance, and the black line shows the retreat. The thickness of the line indicates troop strength — note the casualties taken as indicated by the thick line gradually diminishing, from a start of 400,000 to about 10,000 at the completion of the retreat. The full size version scale is 1 millimeter per 10,000 men.

The bottom section shows the temperature during the retreat, falling from the Fahrenheit equivalent of about 0 to negative 35 degrees. The diagram represents not only a lackluster military strategy but also makes way for an excellent visual management aide.

<u>PROCESS MAP WITH LEFT-TO-RIGHT FLOW</u>

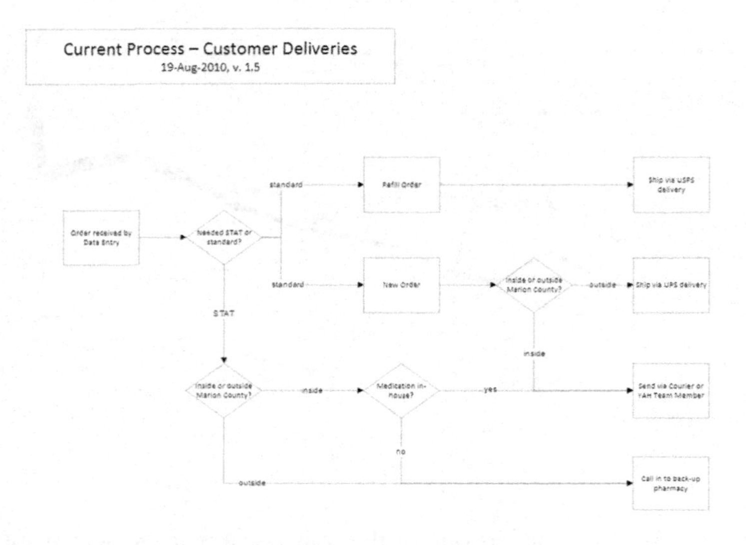

Taiichi Ohno of Toyota introduced the concept of flow, which comes to life in a process map.

In the last chapters, we discussed prioritization of the higher-level business modules. Now that a Level II process map is created, it is time to prioritize the business functions that are the parts of the business module.

After creating a Level II process map, a good next step is to prioritize the business processes, to allow for the effective writing of operating procedures.

I have been successful with two forms of prioritization, a function Lean practitioners will use repeatedly in the quality process. The first is simple; the second is a little more complex.

The simple way is to stratify the projects or elements in a two-by-two matrix, with business benefit on the Y-axis and ease of implementation on the X-axis. That looks something like this:

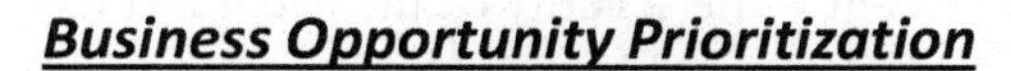

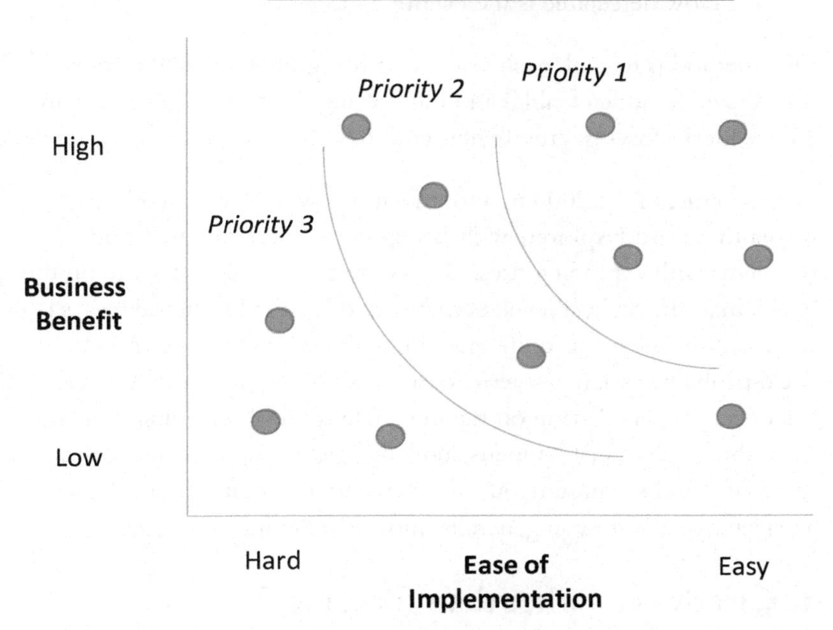

The chart can then be separated into three areas: Priority 1: the top right, being high business benefit, easy to execute; Priority 2: the center area, being a balance of both; Priority 3: the bottom left, being relatively lower business benefit and relatively harder to execute. Using these criteria, you'd start with Priority 1 and work your way down to Priority 3. My experience is that as time progresses and your team gets more engaged with Lean, it is likely they will generate more projects. These will get stratified, and more will be added to Priority 1. It is possible to get so much volume of lower-hanging fruit projects that it might take the company a very long time, if ever, to get to Priority 3 work.

There is a second but more complex way of prioritizing opportunities, and that is known as Failure Modes and Effects Analysis or FMEA. Some Lean people pronounce this "FEE-MA." In FMEA, the team ranks each way of making an error, or "failure mode" using three criteria:

1. What is the likelihood of this happening?
2. What is the severity of the event if it happens?
3. How detectable is the event?

One method is to rank each one 1-5 (5 being the most likely, most severe, and least detectable) and multiplying the figures to get a score. The highest scores get the first attention.

For example, in the 2000 time frame, it was widely reported in the media that Ford Explorers with Bridgestone/Firestone tires had problems with exploding tires. If we were to do a FMEA score on the problem at the highest level, perhaps we'd say the likelihood was a 1- it turns out the even was quite rare although it was in the news a lot. We'd probably assign a severity of a 5- exploding tires with a vehicle full of passengers driving on the interstate is life-threatening. Finally, since the incident just happens suddenly, we'd assign a detectability score of 5, unlike running out of gas, whereby looking at your gas gauge allows you to you generally know it's coming and when.

> "Early on, rather than focusing first on maximizing business benefit, start with ease of implementation.

So, the score is 1x5x5 or 25. Of course this is a guideline, to be taken into account with other factors. In the case of the Ford Explorer, it was a massive public relations issue, and was given top priority. But the example allows me to illustrate the method.

When prioritizing, I have three principles:

1. Start with ease of implementation.
2. Just do it.
3. Give yourself grace.

Let's go back to the prior method of prioritizing, the 2x2 matrix. Early on, rather than focusing first on maximizing business benefit, **start with ease of implementation**; this is particularly helpful in deciding which Lean projects to execute at the beginning of a Lean journey.

A paradigm for prioritization is what I refer to as the New York Times method. I grew up in the New York City area and on Sundays, my dad had a routine of reading the New York Times. Back in those days, before the internet, the local Sunday New York Times was several hundred pages and could approach a thousand pages (the record was in September 1987, with 1,612 pages). It was not uncommon for the Arts and Leisure section alone to be 150 pages. This was the paper of record, and Sunday was the flagship day of the week for newspapers. Reading the Sunday paper was an event.

My dad's method, one of two general approaches, took about two hours and started off on the living room coffee table. He systematically attacked the paper, first eliminating the content he wasn't interested in to make the pile smaller and more relevant. He culled the Real Estate section; since we weren't planning on moving, he had no interest in it. Fortunately, he didn't need a job, and so the "help wanted" section went on the floor under the table. He might have flipped through and scanned article titles in these and similar sections, but soon they found their way onto a discard pile under the table. Dad also quickly dispatched the commercial flyers for retail shops — on the floor they went, and so on.

In this first stage, he winnowed the paper to its critical elements for his interests, a process he seemed to enjoy, and this took, say, 30 minutes. The remaining sections and articles on the coffee table were the important parts of the paper, which he then set about reading. This may have taken 90 minutes. This approach to prioritization directs attention to the lower value-added content first in order to simplify the project going forward, and focus on the higher value-added parts.

An alternative approach would be to say, "Why spend time on lower value-added content first? I'm going to go right to the content I care about — say, business, politics, world news. First, I'll read the valuable areas, and then and only then I might address the lower value-added areas, if I have time."

Each one of these processes is valid. When it comes to selecting which Lean projects to address in a company, the first approach would be to address low-hanging fruit, easy-to-implement projects. These have the advantage of having lower project cycle times and less risk to critical business functions, and can serve as good training projects for team members new to Lean to understand the project in a low-risk manner. In addition, these low-hanging fruit projects may persuade reluctant participants who can help both their company, and more importantly, their daily life as a team member there. They also quickly give team wins and successes to team members, increasing the likelihood that a new Lean initiative gains momentum. Eliminating a section, even a low-value one, is a quick win.

Let's say a company had a small, annoying, wasteful and quite visible problem as seen by the user. In the breakroom, there is a Bunn coffee pot that requires the user to make a full pot — 8 cups of coffee. The problem is that if a team member wants to have a cup of coffee at 4 p.m., and there is an empty pot, the person is required to make a full pot, knowing that the office closes at 5 p.m., and most of the coffee would be wasted. Perhaps there is a Lean project with a solution of using the economical Bunn coffee pot until 2 p.m. and a single-serving Keurig coffeemaker after 2 p.m. The Keurig is more expensive per cup, but not more than wasting most of a pot of coffee. Team members are happy, a small amount of costs is saved, and the Customer need is addressed —problem solved.

However, making coffee is a pretty small problem compared to the other identified continuous improvement opportunities in the firm — becoming efficient at conducting conference calls with the international sales offices, addressing repeated accounting errors, failing the recent safety audit and losing inbound Customer complaint emails.

But these issues are complex, require multifunctional teams with team members from multiple countries, and are often laced with emotion. It is for each company to decide their prioritization, but I have repeatedly seen that the slower approach of first addressing more manageable, easy-to-execute projects first leads to a journey of continuous improvement faster in the long run. This is an application of "going slow to go fast."

The second principle is to just do it. My observation is that when initiating a Lean journey, it is best to get a team together, introduce them to Lean concepts through introductory training, and then learn by doing.

By slogging through a problem, they will apply their prior project management skills and start solving issues that have frustrated them for a long time. The reward at the end of a project — reducing waste, providing personal input to a company process, and getting exposure to the Lean process — will be motivating.

The opposite of the just do it, which I've been pressured to do by some clients, is to exhaustively train everyone in the company before addressing real problems. This training can go deep—the amount of training each person has, and wide—the number of people that are trained. Process improvement is an experiential activity, and a typical reaction is how easy it is after we get started to get results. Like riding a bike or learning to swim, you have to get out there and feel it and do it.

This leads to the third principle, to **give yourself grace**. The first Lean project can be messy, sometimes confusing, and imperfect, but do not let perfection be the enemy of the good and then delay, waiting for the ideal infrastructure, timing or training.

Chapter 6

Writing Operating Procedures

"If you can't describe what you are doing as a process, you don't know what you're doing."

— *W. Edwards Deming, master of continual quality improvement*

I have initiated many process instruction systems for companies. Of the countless formats available, two styles stand out as effective approaches to the journey. The first is an At-A-Glance process document; the second is the Operating Procedure (OP). Use these approaches hand-in-hand if you wish.

Format 1: At-A-Glance Process Document

The At-A-Glance is a one-page document to describe a process. It is more visual than the Operating Procedure, and not as complete. This is the path to 80/20 — getting 80 percent of the value for 20 percent of the effort. This is a good path to get started on for quick traction or for teams that do not have the time to write or read a more complete Operating Procedure, which has more content, detail and breadth. In some cases, the At-A-Glance is the most appropriate, as it is intended to be referred to quickly, and during a process that needs a fast reference.

The following are key elements of an At-A-Glance document:

1. Mission
2. Key steps
3. Outcomes and success criteria
4. Watchouts, key learnings, key insights

Let's examine these sections in detail.

1. **Mission:** It is important to state the key expectations of the document. When I worked for Procter & Gamble the company had a very memo-centric communications culture; if there was no memo-based documentation of a decision, meeting or thought process, it was almost as if the interaction never happened. One unique Procter & Gamble rule was that every memo was to start with the word "This." As in, "This memo describes the Mr. Clean contract manufacturing strategy for 2017." The very first sentence told the reader what the mission and purpose of the document were. After years of reading memos at Procter & Gamble, I can get frustrated when a writer explains his or her purpose halfway down the first page.

   Setting expectations with the user tells them the goal of the At-A-Glance document.

2. **Key Steps:** This is the core section of the At-A-Glance document, and the summary of the operating procedures (OP). Whereas the Operating Procedure exhaustively lists all steps in a process, the At-A-Glance is a concise, scannable version.

   In this section, we want to include just the critical steps. In *The Checklist Manifesto,* Atul Gawande promotes checklists. In his very readable book, he describes the checklist Sully Sullenberger used when he successfully landed the US Airways jet into the Hudson. According to the movie *Sully*, Sullenberger has 208 seconds to land the plane, and both the book and movie depict the pilot referring to a checklist in those critical moments. The deeply experienced pilot knows enough about the spiral-bound checklist book to know it is worth his time. His checklists are to the point: Do process 1, 2 and 3, and then "fly the airplane." The checklist helps the user remember *atypical* tasks 1, 2 and 3, such as the step where the pilot dumps all fuel in the fuel tanks. It is easy to forget a critical step in the heat of the moment. By clearly listing each step in simplified manner, the probability of success by anyone charged with executing that process is dramatically increased. The final task is to execute all things they have been trained in and not to waste time reading or to dilute the key points: "Fly the airplane."

3. **Outcomes and Success Criteria:** This section communicates the desired results. It is critical to know what is expected of you. When your work is handed off to another team member or team, the outcomes and successes are what they expect to receive.

   This section is the objective of the At-A-Glance — accomplish this, and you have succeeded. It defines what Six Sigma would call the "Critical to Customer" attributes.

   In the book *Superforecasting*, by Daniel Gardner and Philip E. Tetlock, the authors discuss military orders. Successful generals such as Eisenhower often gave orders that were proportionally more strategic in nature than tactical. Rather than telling the subordinate what to do, he told the subordinate what they needed to accomplish. "Secure this hill" would be more common than, "At midnight, send 100 troops up the main path, send 50 soldiers to guard your west flank, use anti-tank weapons, and remove all gear that can cause clattering in the night to maintain surprise." The executional details would be left to the discretion of competent, more knowledgeable and possibly more creative commanders on the ground.

   The At-A-Glance document adds outcomes and success criteria to the process steps to identify true success — the outcome rather than the path to take to get there.

4. **Watchouts, Key Learnings, Key Insights:** Consider this a formal mini-chat wall for the process. It is Slack plus Wiki plus Yammer. The author can gather insights from experience and add them here.

Format 2: The Operating Procedure

I think that when properly used, operating procedures are the most essential operations tools for a successful business. They are the house's foundation, and without well-written process instructions, a business stands on shaky ground, at best.

In many companies, there is an execution culture somewhere in the spectrum of from "Just do it!" to "Do it according to process." The "Just do it!" companies get frustrated with rules and procedures — they are disruptors, and perhaps their successful disruptive product is what caused them to be successful. But virtually all companies have repeatable processes that should be executed with minimal variation. As I emphasize throughout this book, standardizing processes does not mean people are robots — rather, their creativity and innovation are better channeled to improve the process than to execute a repeatable process differently each time.

When I owned a pharmacy, we delivered over 3 million prescriptions in nine years. Every 30 seconds, a completed prescription was filled. From inventory to data entry, to billing, to product fulfillment, there were scores of repeatable processes. OPs were critical to ensure quality and drive costs down. Would it have been helpful for a biller to adjudicate 3 million prescriptions 3 million different ways for the sake of variety or "art"? Of course not. I'd much prefer that energy go into continuous improvement.

There's a phrase, commonly cited as originating in the military, that says, "The more you sweat in training, the less you bleed in war." Although this seems not to belong in a discussion of business, this phrase illustrates perfectly the importance of taking the time to perfect one's system. To do so requires a lot of work, but companies that complete that work up front save a lot of work fixing issues that might arise in the future due to a lack of good OP.

Financial radio host and educator Dave Ramsey has a metaphor for debt. He describes being in debt as being in a car at the bottom of a hill. As you start to slowly get things together in your life and pay off your debts, you are slowly climbing the hill in your car. The car has to work hard to keep going, and the going is slow. You are diving uphill and fighting the constant pressure of gravity. However, once you pay off all your debts and begin living debt free, you have crested the hill in your car, and have begun to coast down the other side. As debt payments become saving payments, the car no longer has to work hard to carry you along the road. Gravity is doing all the work, and you are free to relax and go along for the ride. The individual's net worth gains momentum as interest is earned, not paid, and the car coasts.

Similarly, developing a company-wide system of solid OP is a time-consuming undertaking and can certainly be a daunting upfront task. But once the work is done, it is like you have crested the hill in your car — the company is free to no longer worry about the basic processes, and it can coast down the hill to bigger and better things in the future, like continuous improvement. Typically, as the car coast downhill, the costs are reduced as well.

Shortly after college, I remember telling my roommate about a business plan. He suggested I write myself a memo. I questioned his suggestion, and he explained that using the discipline to write down a complex idea like a business plan would add clarity and deeper thought to my idea. I did, and his proposal was a good one. Tt is the same with an operating procedure. It forces the subject matter expert (SME) to think about the process in a structured and logical manner. To tell you a secret, in some cases, I've been in some circumstances where the primary value of an exercise was writing the OP, not in having it used for training or further continuous improvement. I could have tossed the completed OP away — forcing the structured thinking process was what the client really needed. The capture of intellectual property was the bonus.

Doing the work of developing OPs helps businesses find defects in their systems early. If A company reaps the rewards of consistent repeatable processes with well written operational instructions. The company also has a defined benchmark of each process that is unique to the team or organization. Additionally the processes can be used to promote continuous improvement. The company can go from a vicious cycle of errors, rework and frustrated Customers — plus pulling management's attention to fire-fighting — to a virtuous cycle of continuous improvement, with more time to delight Customers.

THE VIRTUOUS PROCESS CYCLE VS. VICIOUS PROCESS CYCLE

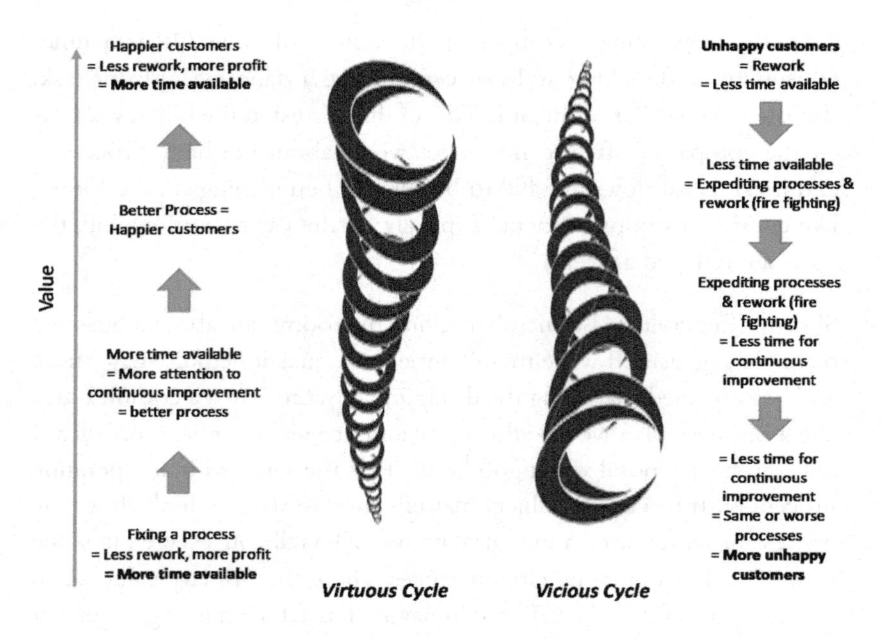

Toyota has a system in place designed to catch defects as soon as possible. Running above assembly lines at Toyota plants are cords like the ones on busses that passengers pull to signal they want to exit the bus. If a factory worker on the line spots a defect in a part, she can pull the cord, which calls attention to her position on the line and halts production progress. This system is called the Andon cord, or Andon, and is designed to remove defective product early in the manufacturing process. Andon gives the workers on the factory floor the ability, and in fact empowers them, to catch defects and other issues and stop them from ever becoming larger problems.

Having good OP in place is like the Andon cord. By first scrutinizing all processes in an organization and then producing process instructions to cover all processes, companies can remove defects in their systems before they ever become a problem.

Rule of Tens

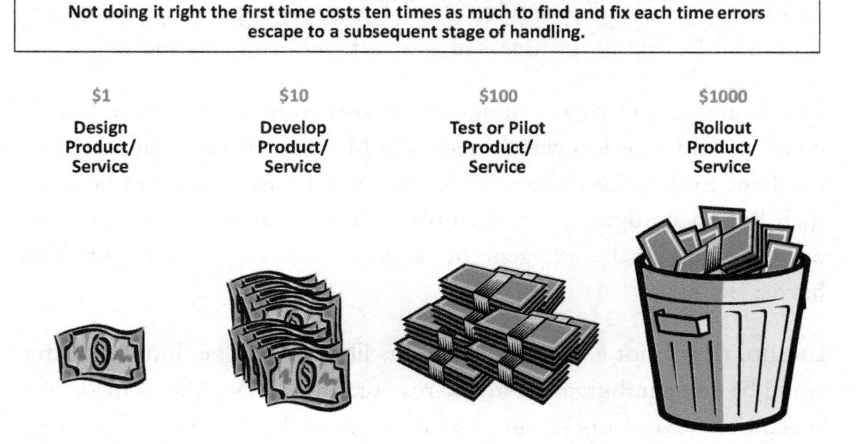

If you don't deal with a defect and nail down your OP during the design phase, time goes by, the defect is allowed to remain in place, and by the time you reach the rollout of your product or service, your costs can multiply tenfold. The illustration above represents this Rule of Tens.

What exactly is the Operating Procedure format?

The Operating Procedure is a list of steps. The list is more elaborate than the checklist or At-A-Glance I described earlier. (Check out my sample template at the end of this chapter.) The Operating Procedure can describe the process of small things, like how to close a retail store or a restaurant at the end of the day, or how to make a sandwich or fold an item of clothing.

The Operating Procedure can also describe the process of massive, important processes within a business, such as building a car on an assembly line (a manufacturing example), or paying team members correctly (a service example). Whether the OP describes small or big processes, they are the same at their core. A snapshot description with a systematic and precise list of actions to follow. . There is a correct way to do every process in every business. The goal of operating procedures is to describe that best process in an exact, deliberate manner.

For example, you might think that if you were a McDonald's team member, and your job was to make Big Macs, the process shouldn't be too hard to describe. You take the two patties and put them between their buns accordingly. You then place all the ordered toppings on top of each patty. Finally, add generous serving of special sauce on top. You have a Big Mac.

But no, this is not a Big Mac. It seems like it could be; but really, this could be any hamburger from any restaurant. The Big Mac is made in a specific way, and operating procedures describe it. The set of steps above leaves out a lot of important information. How long do the patties cook, and at what level of heat? Should the patties go straight from the griddle to the buns, or should they sit for a bit? How much of each topping should go on the sandwich — a small handful of lettuce or a large one; one or two tomato slices; a pinch of diced onion or a handful; two pickles, or is it three? And finally, the special sauce: does it go on the bun or directly on top of the other toppings? Should there be a liberal amount applied or just enough? And once all of this is assembled, should the top bun be squished down onto the burger or gently placed? And what is done with the finished product? It is placed in a box, but then what is done with the box?

Even a process which seems as simple as making a Big Mac can be very complicated and require specific instructions so that it is made correctly. Sure, if Big Macs were made by a looser set of rules, they would probably still taste good most of the time. But an organization must strive for a product that is not only of good quality, but one that is consistently of good quality. Without good operating procedures, the quality of a product like the Big Mac would be subject to considerable variation, and this could be problematic in the long run.

> "An organization must strive for a product that is not only of good quality, but one that is consistently of good quality.

Consistency is a hallmark of McDonald's. I know, as I've eaten at McDonald's across the U.S., Europe and Asia.

Imagine being a consumer and a regular McDonald's Customer around the time of the Big Mac's introduction. You go to McDonald's for lunch one day and decide to try the heavily advertised new flagship sandwich: the Big Mac. Once you've taken your first bite, your whole view of the world changes, and the sandwich is so good that you know you've just bitten off a piece of history. You vow to return to McDonald's soon and get another Big Mac. But when you do return a week later and order the Big Mac, after your first bite, you realize something is off. There's a little too much sauce, and the crunch of the lettuce totally overpowers the rest of the sandwich. You throw your half-eaten Big Mac in the trash as you exit, disappointed. The next time you get a hankering for fast food, you remember your last experience with McDonald's, and suddenly Wendy's seems like a very attractive option.

Because of the variation in the composition of the sandwich in the above scenario, McDonald's has confused a Customer. This is only one of the many losses that could be incurred by a business that lacks good operating procedures. A Starbucks customer certainly expects to receive their order the way they requested it. Now, think about airplane or automobile manufacturers which don't have exact and carefully designed operating procedures – people's lives could be at risk.

We've established the operating procedures are extremely important, but how exactly are they written? The specific process may vary from business to business, but the two roles actively involved in crafting written procedures are the author (the person who writes the procedures with a consistent, company-wide style and appearance) and the subject matter experts (or SMEs).

SMEs are people who have developed deep expertise about the process the authors aim to capture as an operating procedure. The best method is to have an SME that actually performs the process on a daily basis. They know more than anyone about that specific process. The guy or gal in the corner office is typically too detached from many processes to be an effective SME.

Authors usually interview SMEs, asking them to describe in minute details the explicit process they follow each time they perform. An author then takes this data and writes in in a simplified and standardized manner by following pre-established company template. The writing style should be plain and exact. Once the writing is completed, the author shows their version of the process to the SMEs for feedback on correctness. Once correct, the operating procedure is complete.

I have a technical writer on my team who has an uncanny ability to observe any process and return an hour later with OP that are, much to the surprise of the SME, 90 percent accurate. The SME makes some corrections, and the writer returns with 97 percent accurate OP, etc. Typically, the third iteration achieves 100 percent accuracy. We believe we have a current best approach to documenting OPs, as we have written around seven thousand OPs together.

This is a simplified account of the process, and there are often variations in the process from company to company. The important factor here is the use of SMEs to create the operating procedures. They are an invaluable part of the process.

Four Things You Can Do If You Don't Like an Operating Procedure

1. Do it anyway
2. Ask for an exception
3. Work with the Quality Team to improve the process and OP
4. Ignore it and do it the way you want (the only option that is a performance issue)

Consistent execution of operating procedures makes innovation and continuous improvement much easier – especially for complex systems. It is easier to ensure consistency in a centralized and consolidated location and more difficult in a decentralized, remote location. Process variations will always occur. Therefore, team must have a mechanism in place for how to deal with those variations in both centralized or decentralized locations.

FOREVER YOUNG

At-A-Glance
Operating Procedure

MISSION

(why are we doing this, customer expectations, desired outcome, resources required)

PROCESS – CRITICAL STEPS	OUTCOMES / SUCCESS CRITERIA *(why are we doing this, customer expectations, desired outcome)*
• xxx	• xxx

WATCHOUTS, LEARNINGS, KEY INSIGHTS

<u>AT-A-GLANCE OPERATING PROCEDURE SAMPLE</u>

Part Five

Developing a Continuous-Improvement System

Chapter 7

The Corrective and Preventive Action System (CPAS)

"I consider it to be the duty of anyone who sees a flaw in the plan not to hesitate to say so. I have no sympathy with anyone, whatever his station, who will not brook criticism."

— Dwight Eisenhower, in a pre-D-Day strategy meeting, 1944

By implementing Lean Sigma principles on Day 1 at the pharmacy, our team embarked on a decade-long journey of continuous business learning. Before selling the company we received thousands of suggestions from team members and Customers. Most suggestions followed a rapid improvement process (RIP) that addressed and incorporated the surge of intellectual property contributions. Costs went down and quality increased. Customer satisfaction continually climbed.

This quality process is called a corrective and preventive action system (CPAS).

Have you ever ordered a Sprite in a restaurant only to be served a glass of soda water, without the Sprite syrup in it? You take a sip, expecting a sweet, lemony soda, but instead taste a plain soda water. It surprises your palette, like expecting milk and tasting orange juice. What do you do? Typically, you mention it to the waiter, and usually, with a clear Customer-facing defect like that, he will prioritize correcting the defect ahead of his other waiter duties. You have just experienced a corrective action. When defects occur, businesses must perform a corrective action. In such cases, the business has completed the "corrective" aspect of CPAS.

The key to breakout quality companies, however, is when the company or organization follows up a corrective action with a preventive action, the "P" in CPAS. The "prevention" step is a way to make sure the error only happens once, and that the process is changed in the future to reduce or eliminate the likelihood of it happening again. In many cases, CPAS is an action performed in a way that not only maintains but also grows Customer satisfaction.

REAL WORLD: Sprite syrup deficit leads to a better process

Imagine that the dinner seating in a restaurant is over. It's after midnight, and all the Customers have gone. The five waiters and waitresses are sitting in chairs in a circle after performing their after-hour duties. They're having a drink and debriefing about the day. They have over 25 years of restaurant service experience among them. Perhaps the leader asks, "based on this evening, what are ways we could have improved our service?" One person tells the story about the Sprite.

"OK, that's a good one," the leader says, perking up a little. "We ran out of Sprite syrup in the soda machine. In the future, how can we prevented that from happening in the first place?" she asks. A hush falls over the team as they sip drinks and think.

"Behind the soda machine are tanks of syrup, one for each style," one person says. "I suppose we could have a meter on each tank, like the one I have on my propane tank at home. When I have people over for a barbeque, I always check the level the day before so I know if I have to buy a replacement tank and have it ready."

"What if we always have a replacement tank ready for each flavor?" another person suggests. "But currently it's a pain to change over our tanks — we need a wrench, and I don't have time during our peak hours to do it. But I know our sister restaurant has more modern couplers that allow the user to 'hot swap' tanks in under a minute. We could change the couplers that attach the tanks to the syrup lines, and then we can do a changeover quickly." Great thoughts, and then a third waiter pipes up.

"Maybe we can have the supplier, the Coke guy who changes the tanks, be responsible for that, and ask him to make sure we don't run out," she says. Another good idea, and they keep coming.

"How about if we put each tank on a bathroom scale? When the tanks are getting low, we'll know at what weight we need to be watching it and have a tank ready."

Another says, "This probably a dumb suggestion …" In Lean, this sentence start is a sure sign that a very good suggestion may be coming because some of the best preventive actions are the simplest and most obvious. Does a pilot in her preflight checklist check the fuel gauge to ensure the plane has enough fuel to get to the next destination? Yes, always. Does a surgeon ask the patient if she is operating on the left arm or the right arm? The good ones do. Back to the restaurant. She continues, "… what if before our big-volume nights, on Fridays and Saturdays, I volunteer to check each soda tap with a Dixie cup to see if the level seems like it's getting low?" Perfectly logical suggestion.

This conversation continues. Without building a new computer system or spending lots of money on consultants, the experienced team, with a little bit of focused discussion, comes up with half-a-dozen solid countermeasures to address the issue. Someone writes the agreed-upon suggestion on an index card, and they execute a few processes to get started, like talking to the syrup supplier. The service team stays disciplined for three weeks to get into the habit of implementing the processes, in a training mode. With all of those countermeasures implemented, would the likelihood of committing the defect again be reduced by 100 percent? Perhaps not, but perhaps it could be reduced by 80-90 percent — pretty good for a few tired waiters and waitresses at the end of a shift, with a continuous improvement culture.

As a postscript to the story, now imagine that at the next regional meeting the general manager of each location in this chain of restaurants shares their best practices and they get implemented region-wide. The sphere of influence grows.

To initiate a CPAS system, find room for improvement.

The CPAS process starts with collecting opportunities to continuously improve. This can be done with a CPAS form. A few examples follow. I give these forms in half-page pads to every team member with whom I work. As they go about their work day, they identify areas of improvement, capture them on a form for a central person (such as a quality manager or team leader) to collect. They can track them on a spreadsheet, in a deck of forms, or on the wall of a war room. The team can then prioritize them and execute rapid improvement process (RIP) events, discussed in Chapter 8.

As I've mentioned before, the CEO far removed from the line and sitting in the corner office usually doesn't have the depth of real-time knowledge cultivated from performing processes, so they cannot generate these ideas alone. The ideas must come from the people actually doing the work. The person who runs the CNC machine in a machine shop for 40 hours a week will have a richer, different level of understanding on the details, and therefore the opportunities, of the work related to the machine than anyone else.

This is the purpose of the corrective and preventive action system. It's a mouthful, but CPAS – more or less – is like an optimized suggestion box for Lean production. When someone has an idea to improve their team's procedure, or their building's, or the whole business', she can run it through CPAS; if it's a good enough idea, or points out a serious enough flaw, it will result in a Rapid Improvement Process (RIP) and an optimized process for the company. Team members from every level can help an organization innovate using CPAS.

The quantity and quality of generated suggestions grows significantly when CPAS cards are actively supported. Companies can create a continuous-improvement culture by rewarding CPAS suggestions by instituting a Lean belt system, offering cash rewards or integrating participation in performance reviews. After a few years, our pharmacy typically had more than 500 CPAS ideas that could be used by the quality manager for content for her weekly RIP. We did a RIP a week for almost a decade.

A STANDARD CPAS FORM

CPAS CARD *v1.0 mmm yy* Name:______________

Team: ☐ Operations ☐ Leadership ☐ Finance ☐ ______

Owner, Date

Priority: Low | Med | High | Super High

Urgency: High | Medium | Low

Business Benefit: High | Medium | Low

Ease of Implement-ation: Easy | Medium | Hard

Growth Impact (Drive Sales): High | Medium | Low

Situation

Complication

Required Attendees

A Specific CPAS Form for the Pharmacy

The CPAS form above is a generic, but effective one. It fits on half a sheet of paper and allows the user to compete the form with ease from work his station. They name the defect, identify the team that would be involved in analyzing the issue, and then complete a few checklists. They first assess the holistic sense of the overall priority. Then they score it based on the urgency, business benefit, and their guess of how easy it would be to address the problem. The last bubble assesses if this might impact growth— in other words, would addressing this situation help sales? For example, eliminating a product defect would directly improve growth, but reducing clutter in the office supply closet probably would not.

CPAS Documentation Form

CPAS = Corrective & Preventive Action System

Date:		Reported By:	
Facility:		Patient:	
Rx Number:		Contact:	
Severity Level:			
☐ Level 1a	Dispensing defect, customer-facing, wrong drug	☐ Level 2	Dispensing defect, internal-facing
☐ Level 1b	Dispensing defect, customer-facing, wrong quantity	☐ Level 3	Non-dispensing, customer-facing
☐ Level 1c	Dispensing defect, customer-facing, wrong dose (strength)	☐ Level 4	Non-dispensing, internal-facing
☐ Level 1d	Dispensing defect, customer-facing, delivery issue	☐ Level 5	Waste issue
☐ Level 1e	Dispensing defect, customer-facing, other	☐ Level 6	IT Systems issue
		☐ Level 7	Customer recognition (Not a quality issue; Young at Heart went above and beyond to meet a customer need)

Issue Description
(Please provide detail adequate to fully understand issue being documented)

Team Involved:

Pharmacists ____ Pharmacy Ops ____ Materials Handling ____ Data Entry ____ Billing ____ Other ________

The image above is another example of a CPAS documentation form. This is one way to put the CPAS into practice. This example is for a pharmacy — it is highly specialized — and examples from other businesses will likely look significantly different, but the principle is the same across all fields. The form provides a standardized way to report an issue that occurred and include all of relevant details.

In this CPAS form, any reported issue is assigned a severity level based on the type of error that occurred. For example, a Level 1 error is a Customer-facing dispensing error, such as wrong dose, wrong quantity or wrong drug. Fortunately, we had very few of these. A Level 2 error was a dispensing error that got caught before reaching the Customer, such as in a pharmacist quality check. A Level 2 would be like the Federal Aviation Administration requiring an airline to report a "near miss," or two airplanes that flew too close to each other but did not collide. An example of a non-dispending error may be a billing error — something that didn't affect the drug itself. This leveling system helps prioritize which issues to deal with first if multiple issues occur at the same time. Again, this form is industry and business specific, so a custom form can be designed for any industry.

After collecting CPAS data, the next step is the Rapid Improvement Process or RIP. We'll discuss RIPs next.

Chapter 8

The Rapid Improvement Process (RIP)

"I've missed more than 9,000 shots in my career. I've lost almost 300 games. Twenty-six times, I've been trusted to take the game-winning shot and missed. I've failed over and over and over again in my life. And that is why I succeed."

— *Michael Jordan, former basketball player who led the Chicago Bulls to six NBA championships and won the Most Valuable Player Award five times*

The major tenet of the Lean system is continual improvement. This means never settling, always striving for more and recognizing that improvement is nearly always possible. Lean practitioners know that the ability to improve is as important an asset as any other.

Former NFL coach Bill Parcells once shared insight into his decision-making process regarding draft prospects. He said that if he were considering two different running backs, both of whom could run a 4.5-second 40-yard dash, the player with worse running form would be the one he would want to draft. This is because he saw the improvement potential in the player with worse form. Both players ran fast 40-yard dashes, but the player with poor form could run even faster if he improved his form under Parcells' coaching. The other player had less room to improve. Between two processes that do the same job with similar effectiveness, if one is much less organized, Lean tells us to embrace the challenge of improving processes.

> "Between two processes that do the same job with similar effectiveness, if one is much less organized, Lean tells us to embrace the challenge of improving processes.

What sort of improvements can be made to a disorganized or poorly designed process? In order to know this for sure, we need to know what needs to be improved. If you don't know what is broken or if something is broken, there's no way to fix it.

The goal of Lean production is to minimize waste. I discussed waste in the first chapter, but I'll go into more detail here, before we move on to discuss the process for fixing a wasteful aspect of a business.

THE SEVEN TYPES OF WASTE

1. Processing
2. Rework
3. Waiting
4. Motion
5. Over Production
6. Transportation
7. Inventory and Storage

Let's break down each kind of waste individually.

1. **Processing:** Processing waste is produced when you take more time than necessary to process something. An example of this might be traffic on a highway. The city is experiencing processing waste because it is not moving vehicles as efficiently as possible.

2. **Rework:** This is waste that occurs when you must do something more times than necessary due to poor processes. My wife once received an email invitation to an event in downtown Indianapolis. In the email, there were two dates listed: one was the registration deadline, and the other was the date of the event. The dates were not clearly labeled. As a result, she ended up coordinating childcare then driving 30 minutes to the event only to find that no one else had showed up. She had arrived at the event location on the registration deadline instead of the actual event date. So, she had to come home and then return three days later to actually attend the event. She performed the work of driving to the event twice. This is rework.

3. **Waiting:** Waiting is ubiquitous and often overlooked, but waiting around for things to get done is wasteful. Customer waiting is the most common kind of waste, but it also occurs within organizations and can often be just as costly.

   One example of an organization attempting to minimize waiting is Kroger's Six Sigma initiative, where at each register line in the store, there should be a maximum of one person checking out and one person waiting behind them. That's all. If there are any more than this in any of the lanes, new lanes need to be opened to open revenue bottlenecks at registers by pulling staff from other functions such as the deli and restocking. What's the point of advertising and fully stocking shelves if a frustrated customer with a full shopping cart leaves in frustration just as they are about to purchase groceries and contribute to profits?

   Another initiative focused on reducing wait times was carried out by the Indiana Bureau of Motor Vehicles (BMV) I recently set my stopwatch on my iPhone to time my wait from taking a number to being called at my local BMV: 3.4 seconds.

REAL WORLD: Turning the tables on your doctor

I remember once I was waiting at the doctor's office for a routine check-up appointment. One of the nurses gave the form to fill out on the clipboard like always, but this time I actually read through some of the contracts to sign. In one of them, there was a line that stated there was a $25 fee for showing up late to an appointment. This irked me, because it was a one-way street and shouldn't have been. So I modified the contract so that the specific stipulation worked mutually, making it required that if I had to wait for my doctor when I arrived on time to my appointment, the office would have to pay me $25.

I completed the form with this one modification and returned it to the nurse. She flipped through it back at her desk, and when she arrived at my modification, she seemed puzzled and began discussing it in hushed tones with a doctor who had walked by. She eventually came back to me and handed me the page containing the form I had modified and said that I didn't have to fill that one out. Even a $25 cost was too much for them to risk!

4. **Motion:** This is another kind of waste that is often hidden. Examples might be motion in a factory if an assembly line is poorly designed and consecutive systems are not nearby each other. Motion waste could be at home, if you search all over your garage to find a tool and just end up driving to Home Depot to buy a new one.

5. **Over-production:** Let's say I'm on my way home from work, and my wife calls and tells me we're out of milk and to please buy a gallon of milk on the way home. Thinking I'm being clever, I buy 10 gallons of milk to save us trips later on. Of course, my family can't drink 10 gallons of milk before much of it spoils, so we will end up throwing out a lot of unused milk. This is overproduction waste. Over production also leads to excess inventory. Excess inventory is usually a costly, bad thing. More on that later.

6. **Transportation:** Excess travel is never good. Back at the Indiana BMV, Customers used to be required to physically go to a bricks-and-mortar location to renew licenses and do other basic clerical tasks. Now, many of these these functions are completed online, successfully eliminating much of the transportation waste in the system.

7. **Inventory and Storage:** Excess inventory is inherently bad. It is expensive to buy, and doing so ties up cash. It can result in shrinkage or theft, unplanned obsolescence (like stocking up on 10 years of Motorola cell phone batteries—yes, I know they don't make them anymore), and spoilage (like the milk example). It is also expensive to store. Finally, motion is often wasted searching through warehouses full of inventory, looking for something specific. Refer to the story of Taiichi Ohno and the milk cartons in Chapter 1 for a better way to do inventory.

These different kinds of waste descriptions describe the potential problems facing organizations. They can overlap, though. A simpler way of looking at waste is via Taiichi Ohno's philosophy that there are three types of waste. In Japanese, these are "muda," "muri" and "mura." Muda is any non-value-added activity, as described above. Muri describes the overburdening of people or equipment. Mura is unevenness. These three encompass the seven kinds of waste discussed. With this knowledge, no problem should go unnoticed in an organization.

The Lean improvement process, or the rapid improvement process, succeeds because of its unique, non-traditional approaches to problems. The table below cites a few examples.

Traditional vs. Lean Improvement Approaches

Situation	Traditional	Lean
Bottleneck in factory	Buy a bigger machine	Free-up bottlenecks
Car stuck in traffic	Buy a faster car	Plan a new route
Office supplies sale	Buy in bulk	Buy what is needed
Need for more copier capacity	Buy a larger copier	Buy more small copiers
Need car oil change	Drop off car with dealer	Drive through Jiffy Lube

As you can see from the examples above, many traditional improvement approaches seem to be more focused on patching up holes in localized areas of their processes, rather than focusing on redesigning the system to avoid stress points. I've read Eliyahu Goldratt's book *The Goal* in every job I've had and was even able to take a class from him several years ago. His fable on bottlenecks describes the optimization of a system very well.

One recommendation from Lean approaches is that processes are best improved at a manual level first (i.e., the simplest form of the process), before considering any attempts at automation or other technological remedies. For example, if you have a poorly designed process then attempt to fix it by automating it, you are essentially just polishing a turd. The underlying process is still bad despite the expensive "fix" of automation.

An absurd example of this, as seen in the above table, is like someone who buys a fast sports car because they are constantly stuck in traffic on their way to work. The sports car may be faster than other cars on an open road with no speed limits or traffic, but in a traffic jam, every car is subjected to the same situation, no matter their horsepower or handling capabilities. In that situation, the better approach would be to try to find a new route that avoids the traffic all together or change departure times — that is, to design a new process before spending money on machinery.

A good illustration of the process for redesigning a process as part of a RIP follows:

The System Development Spectrum

High Cost
Stable
Inflexible
Slow to Innovate

Enterprise System

Internal Application

Access

Excel

Low Cost
Unstable
Flexible
Fast to Innovate

This graphic shows how organizational software tools can track process improvement. Start by optimizing that process at the entry level, say, the Microsoft Excel level, which is a low-cost, high-flexibility system that allows lay tech people to quickly innovate. Though flexible, this level is also very unstable long-term. You can bring in new software tools at each level as the process is perfected, even approaching the level of using an Enterprise System where you once used Excel. Here, you are using a high-cost, low-flexibility system, but it is one that is very stable and scalable.

Moving up this tool spectrum can optimize your processes along the way, and is a minimally viable product (MVP) approach. This hearkens back to our earlier discussion about the cost of addressing defects and how it rises over time. If the above development system is used, defects will be caught early, and the extra cost of addressing them later will never be incurred. Eric Ries' *Lean Startup* is the go-to reference to learn more about MVPs in an entrepreneurial setting.

Corrective and Preventive Action (CPAS) Card

Rapid improvement process begins with the Standard CPAS Form (See Chapter 7). If you recall in Chapter 1, we discussed the issue Brian has with finding his keys every morning, and that he used a RIP to solve this problem. If Brian had this problem as part of a team at a business, he would have grabbed one of these sheets and filled it out before attempting to make any changes or alleviate the problem.

Say Brian is the owner of the above CPAS Card, and that he is using it for his problem with losing his keys. First, he should fill in the spaces for team (him and his wife, here) and owner (himself). The next step is to describe the situation (in the box titled situation, of course). In this box, Brian will write two or three short paragraphs explaining the "why" of the project at hand.

Barbara Minto, in her book *The Pyramid Principle*, lays out a basic communication framework: *situation, complication, answer*. A situation is a fact that no one disputes. In Brian's case, it is that he spends twenty minutes every morning looking for his keys.

Next, Brian fills out the box titled complication. A complication is a description of what exactly is causing the problem. In Brian's case, it is that spending twenty minutes looking for keys every morning makes him late to work often.

However, the cause of a problem isn't always as obvious as it is in the case of Brian. One method used to explore the possible causes of an issue is using a fishbone diagram.

Fishbone Diagram

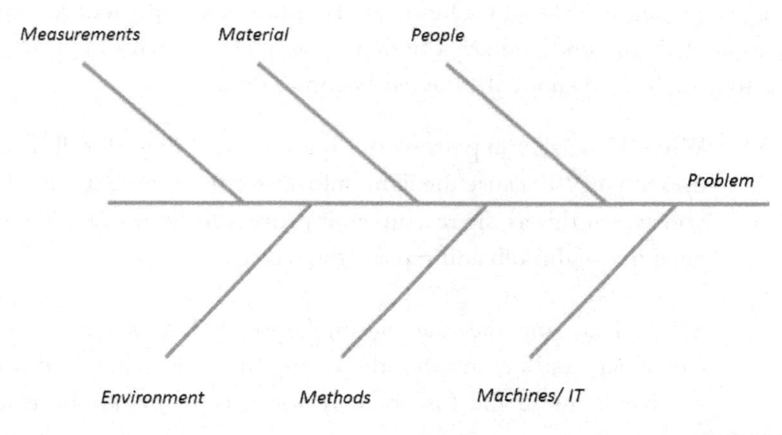

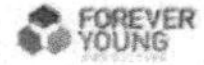

To use this diagram, start at the right side with your problem, and move through all the branches, or bones, while considering all the things that might be causing your problem. Let's say that your problem is that your car won't start. So, you move leftward down the diagram and look at the Machines/IT branch. At this branch you might consider and check for such causes as your engine's starter being broken, your battery cables being corroded, or your battery being dead.

If you consider these options and none of them seems to be the issue, move on to the next branch: People. Perhaps you have used the wrong key or haven't been depressing the brake pedal when attempting to start your car. If people aren't the issue, continue leftward on to Methods, Material, Environment and Measurement. Eventually you will find the cause or causes of your problem.

After the process helps you identify the actual issue you can fix the root cause, which, as previously addressed, is always better than addressing a symptom before moving on.

Ask Why Five Times

Another way to find the root cause of an issue is to ask WHY five times. This is something Taiichi Ohno of Toyota always preached. For example, let's pretend you are a bartender at a TGI Fridays on a busy Saturday night, and suddenly, the bar becomes dark.

1. **Why?** You ask you patrons this question and they all roll their eyes at you. "Because the light bulb above the bar went out." If you accept this as the reason, your process to fix it would be to get a new lightbulb and replace the old one.

2. **Why?** But why did the lightbulb go out? You call in an electrician, and he says that the wrong fuse was being used for the bar lights in the fuse box. If you accept this as the true reason the bar went dark, your process to fix the problem would be to replace the fuse.

3. **Why?** If you ask why the wrong fuse was used and investigate that problem, you find that all the different fuses look remarkably similar and are therefore easy to confuse during installation. Your fix for this problem might be to get new, color-coded fuses installed to make installation much more straightforward. Because all the fuses in the restaurant are improved, you may get a report that lighting in the kitchen has just suddenly improved!

This example ends after asking why three times, but we could continue. If you stopped asking why after the first time, you would have changed the light bulb, but since the wrong fuse was being used, it would have continued to frequently go dark in the bar, as every lightbulb would go out eventually due to the incorrect fuse.

If you had stopped asking why after the second time, you would have changed the fuse, and the lights would have been fine for a while, but the next time the fuses needed to be changed, it would be likely that a mistake would be made, and the incorrect fuse would again be installed, causing the original problem to recur in the future. In addition, the extra *why* allowed the problem solver to have an impact beyond the bar area.

As you can see, by asking why numerous times (in this case, three, but this will obviously vary) you able to get to the heart of an issue, closer to solving it in the most efficient way. Every time you ask why about a problem, the impact you cause by a solution will become greater. Your sphere of influence grown with each layer of "why."

After going through one of these processes to find an issue's root cause, (which you discovered via a RIP sheet), you can complete the rest of the sheet with your team, deciding on priority, ease of implementation, urgency, business benefit and growth impact.

Congrats! You have filled out a RIP and initiated a potential Lean continuous improvement solution.

As discussed, a wonderful and typical outcome of RIPs is the reduction of waste. Often, in the short term, this means fewer people needed to execute a function, such as bill processing, machining or staffing a call center.

Let's say that prior to working on a Lean initiative, it takes four people on a team to get the work done. Then, after going through a rapid improvement process, which identifies areas that are critical to the Customer, calls out non-value added activities, analyzes root causes of non-value added activities, and implements countermeasures, it now takes three people to perform the same function.

What an accomplishment! What a success. What is the one thing management can do to kill the golden goose? The answer is to cut costs by laying off the fourth person. If you do so, congratulations, you likely have executed your first and last Lean project at your company. You will have created a strong disincentive to reduce waste, and waste will be your partner for a long time. Think word will not get around? Think you can move piles of sand around to disguise a layoff? It is highly unlikely to work.

Instead, consider some of the following adjustments to the organizations:

- transfer that one team member has requested for years — either to a new team, a new geography or a new function.
- promote someone.
- Add capacity to training, to 5-S (the method for organizing a work space for efficiency and effectiveness) or to sales.
- If you can't find anywhere to put extra people, move them to the Lean team for six months, and have them contribute to reducing more waste in the company;

But above all, don't punish people's livelihoods as a consequence of doing something good for the company. With this in mind, don't only strive to improve and make a single process great. Instead, you must strive to do something great in the big picture.

> "You must strive to do something great in the big picture.

There's an old anecdote about President Abraham Lincoln that Seapoint Center founder Jesse Lyn Stoner describes on her website.

I'm paraphrasing here:

He used to slip out of the White House one evening a week to listen to the sermons of Dr. Phineas Gurley at the New York Avenue Presbyterian Church. He tried to do so without being noticed, as he was the president after all, and people would be more than excited to see him in person. So, he often sat in the minister's study, just adjacent to the sanctuary where Dr. Gurley delivered his sermons.

One Sunday, walking home from that week's service, one of Lincoln's aides asked him what he thought of the sermon. Lincoln replied that he thought Dr. Gurley had delivered the sermon eloquently, and that the content of it was excellent. The aide replied, "So you thought it was an excellent sermon?"

"No," Lincoln replied. "The content was excellent, and he delivered it with eloquence and grace, but Dr. Gurley forgot the most important ingredient to a sermon. He forgot to ask us to do something great."

Take Lincoln's message to heart as you work through RIPs. Don't only strive for great content. Strive to incite greatness from others and from yourself.

Rapid Improvement Process Worksheets, or RIP Sheets

A3: EDK Rationalization

Owner: Jane smith

v. 1.0, dd mm yy

Business Case

- The Emergency Drug Kit (EDK) configuration is outdated. Reconfiguring the EDK contents will reduce inventory, spoilage, inventory tracking complexity, simplify the EDK maintenance process, and make EDKS more useful to the customer
- When FRX originally configured the EDKs in 3Q04, we took a superset of all the individual EDKs of the 30 MMM homes. We now need to see what drugs should be added to reduce stats and what drugs should be removed to reduce waste.

Countermeasures	*Owner*	*Date*	*Status*
• Generate a database with the current inventory of EDK content, sorted by kit and cost	PZ	15 July	
• Generate an EDK usage report	BJH	15 July	
• Add usage to EDK inventory database	PZ	22 July	
• Create a database of what drugs have been ordered using stat deliveries	PZ	22 July	
• Create a recommendation of drugs to be added and removed	PZ	29 July	
• Create a plan to systematically collect old EDKs and reconfigure them to new ones	PZ	29 July	
• Review with leadership	PZ	5 Aug	
• Execute plan	AEG	12 Aug	

Current Condition

- EDKs are not based on actual usage
- Some drugs in the EDKs are not being used and should be removed
- Some drugs that should be in the EDKs are not currently included and should be added
- The size of the EDKs is arbitrary and should be evaluated, taking into account the reduction of stats and the addition of inventory and the work to maintain them

Target Condition

- EDKs are based on actual usage
- All drugs in the EDKs are necessary
- No drugs that are not in the EDKs are omitted
- The size of the EDKs is strategically determined

I use a RIP sheet that is very simple. It is similar to an A3 worksheet that many Lean practitioners use. The term "A3" derives from the European paper size that is closest to the US 11-by-17-inch size, and was the original paper size Lean people used to create a one-page project plan — the name A3 stuck.

There are countless A3 designs available. The RIP sheet, above, has four simple quadrants. I like my A3s to be implementable by anyone in the organization regardless of work experience or education level, so I keep them simple. I'm not trying to impress people with complexity. The following explains the sections, starting at the top left and working counter-clockwise:

1. **Business Case:** This section is up to three paragraphs long. It describes what is going on and what the issue is. Try to keep it so simple and high level that you can use this to explain the situation to your mom or dad, or someone with no familiarity of the company or problem.

2. **Current Condition:** This quadrant contains three to five bulleted items of conditions that describe the situation today, all aspects of the business you want to change. They are statements, such as, "There is a 5-minute wait to get a table at our restaurant."

3. **Target Condition:** These are bulleted items corresponding to the current condition that describes the future state of your business. For example, "The Customer is greeted and seated immediately upon arrival to the concierge station."

4. **Countermeasure, or Action Plan:** This is the plan of how you will get from the current condition to the target condition. There are four columns: countermeasures (or tasks), owner, date the task is due, and status. Status can be one of the following: not started, WIP (work in progress), done or late; or green (no issues), yellow (some issues) or red (major issues). This section is intended to be a summary of the project plan. There could be a larger project plan with more details that the project leader may have, but this is an executive summary for use by the team.

In my experience, at first some managers may want a very detailed project plan that cannot fit into this section. However, if you do enough RIPs — say, one-a-week — managers will spend more time writing project plans than doing the work. The objective is not to have beautiful documentation, but to get business results, so I'd keep the maintenance and administration of RIP sheets to a reasonable level.

The A3s, since they are only one page, are useful tools to post to a wall for a RIP wall. When the RIP is completed take the sheet off of the wall or move it to a completed section. In the past, I have copied completed RIP sheets onto green paper to show that the work is complete.

Part Six

The Journey and Striving for Perfection

Chapter 9

The Path Forward and the PDCA Cycle

"Just remember to learn your craft. Even before you start to think of yourself as an artist, learn your craft."

— *Steven Spielberg*

Lessons From Tugboats and Fire and Forget Missiles

After managing teams and people for a couple of decades, I have occasionally had to have the "barge and tugboat" talk. When a barge is pulled by a tugboat up the river, it is a slow and arduous process. This is how it works: The tugboat slowly heads upstream. The coiled slack in the towrope between the two craft slowly gets stretched out as the slack goes away. At some point, the rope gets taut, and the tugboat starts pulling the barge upstream. At this point, they are moving at the same pace, always at the speed of the tugboat and with the tugboat expending all of the energy to keep them moving.

Now, if the tugboat stops pulling, the barge keeps going for a while because of momentum, but slowly comes to a halt. As a team member are you a barge? Does your manager have to keep checking on you and prodding you to hit your objectives? What an expenditure of energy and responsibility that tugboat has — it has to move itself and you.

The opposite is the "fire and forget" missile. In World War II and Vietnam, bombs were "dumb." A bomber with a target often had to drop its bombs, and then confirm that the target was hit before flying away. That was dangerous, as the extended presence in enemy territory and the bombing activity often alerted the enemy to shoot back.

Later, "smart" missiles were created, also called "fire and forget" missiles, using guidance systems such as those guided by lasers. The pilot released the missile with the utmost of confidence that it would hit the target. After releasing the missile, the pilot was able to turn around and move on to the next objective.

I encourage my team members to strive to be that fire and forget missile. Your manager gives you an objective and moves on to the next task, fully confident you will deliver. What a difference in energy and confidence compared to that of the barge.

Be a fire and forget missile, not a barge.

One of the cornerstones of Lean production is the concept of the PDCA cycle. You may remember this graphic from way back in Chapter 1 of this book:

Memory refreshed? I touched on this topic, but — like all things Lean — this concept needs a little more explanation, as it is critical.

Plan, Do, Check, Act. The impact of following the PDCA cycle is large and far-ranging, which is why this concept is one of the cornerstones of

Lean production. Rather than go through each work of the cycle individually, like I have done for many concepts in this book, I'm going to touch on various concepts and ideas that are either the result of, or which illustrate, the PDCA cycle in practice.

Incremental Improvement

TWO APPROACHES TO IMPROVEMENT

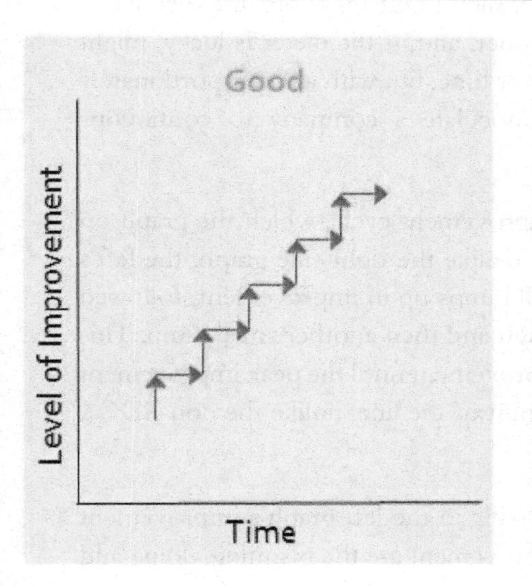

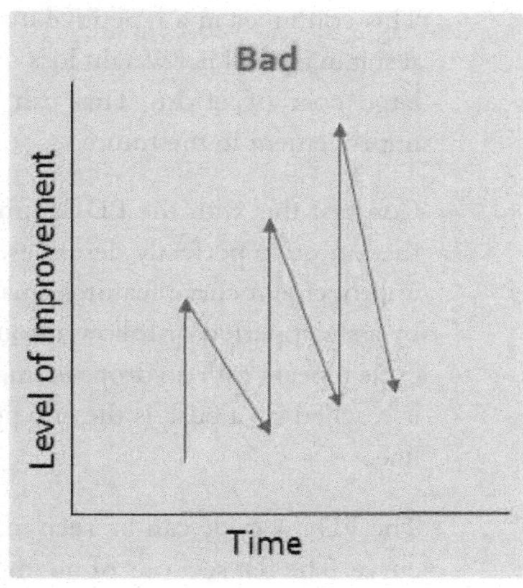

These two graphs visually represent improvement over time. On the left, improvement under PDCA is described. On the right is non-standardized, non-PDCA improvement. The improvement curve of the graph on the right is characterized by large improvements followed by almost immediate drops in improvement. Over time, the real improvement made is actually incremental, even though at the improvement curve's peak, the level of improvement may be very high. This is due to lack of follow-though by the organization, team, department or entity this chart hypothetically represents.

Improvement is recognized as a good thing by this hypothetical entity, but if it is does not have follow-through or lacks planning, checking or sustaining, at important points in the process, the large jumps in improvement are not sustainable in the long run.

A good example of this kind of improvement, also known as the wrong kind, is a fad diet, such as the Atkins or grapefruit diet. These diets, when followed, might lead to large drops in weight in a short period of time. However, they are so restrictive and out of balance that most people can't follow them for very long, and so after initially losing weight in the first week or two of the diet, the person following it breaks and returns to their normal habits for a week or two before realizing that they've gained it all back, at which point they start the diet again. This continues in a repetitive manner, and, if the dieter is lucky, might result in a small net weight loss over time, but with a disproportionately large cost of effort. This can inoculate a company to continuous improvement in the future.

Contrast this with the PDCA improvement cycle, which the graph on the left quite perfectly describes. Unlike the right-side graph, the left's improvement curve features small jumps up in improvement, followed by a short period of follow-through and then another small jump. This cycle repeats with no drops in improvement until the peak improvement is reached — a peak is the end point of the line, unlike the non-PDCA line.

The PDCA cycle can be seen visually in the left graph's improvement curve. The flat sections of no improvement are the planning, doing and checking stage. If we were to zoom in on the flat sections of the graph, we might see tiny peaks and valleys describing the planning phase, the first attempt at improvement following planning (characterized as either a peak or a valley) and then returning to the initial level of improvement in the checking stage, when the gains in the doing stage are standardized or the losses incurred are remedied.

If we zoom back out from the flat sections, we see each flat section (PDC section) is followed by a small quick jump up in improvement. This is the action stage. In the PDC stage we may not see visible improvement, but this phase ensures the stable and incremental improvement we see in the action stage. And this improvement does not drop. The PDC part of the cycle also ensures that the improvements made are sustainable ones, which is why they are small. This all adds up to small, incremental steps up, which over time add up to a large amount of improvement overall.

When you have an infection, and take a ten-day course of antibiotics, the doctor tells you to finish your entire course of medicine, even if you appear to improve dramatically in the first half of the ten-day period. The second five days of the medicine therapy is the follow-through, which ensures the bacteria will not reappear, and you will not make the bacteria resistant to your medicine in the future. So it is with the PDCA process.

If we follow the analogy from above of losing weight, while non-PDCA plans might include highly restrictive diets, PDCA-like plans for losing weight could include small improvement such as:

- Walking 1 mile every day.
- Slowly decreasing the levels of sugar and cream in your morning coffee.
- Taking the stairs over the elevator whenever the choice arises.
- Gradually cutting back on overall calories consumed.

All of these weight-loss plans are easily followed. They don't include massive sacrifices like the grapefruit diet might. They are simply little things to be done every day which, on a long enough timeline, will result in weight loss. When I managed a pharmacy, we focused on completing just one RIP (Rapid Improvement Process) per week, sometimes two. By the end of nine years we had often completed over 450 RIPs and were a much better business because of it. This is the idea of PDCA at work.

Small Batch Sizes

A concept that is tied closely to incremental improvement via PDCA is the idea of small batch sizes. This is basically the idea of producing only a few items at a time, physical or conceptual, so that they can be more easily checked for quality and improved upon. Taiichi Ohno developed a system of small batch sizes called single piece flow, which worked about how it sounds: single item batches. This is an extreme version of the concept, but it shows that when it comes to batch sizes, smaller is often better.

REAL WORLD: Making copies, not mistakes

Let's imagine that you are making a presentation. It's a 50-page PowerPoint document, and you need to make 25 copies to hand out to your future audience. You have 10 minutes until you're front and center, so you head to the copy machine, drop in all 50 pages of the presentation and hit start.

But let's pause for a moment. What you have just done may be a bad idea. Your copying plan can be fraught with risk. It may not necessarily seem that way, but many things could go wrong. For example:

- The copier might run out of paper or staples when you only have 10 copies done.
- There could be a paper jam.
- There could be a smear on the glass, ruining every page.

If any one of these things happened in the middle of your 25-set marathon of a 50-page presentation, you could be in trouble. If you instead follow the principles of PDCA, and in doing do use small batch sizes, the risk of this is greatly reduced.

Here's a better plan: Print only one copy at first and check for any abnormalities. Make any needed adjustments, and then run the rest of the copies in groups of five sets, checking each batch for quality. The risk in this strategy is much less than your all-at-once all-in plan, and the quality of your copies will invariably be better. It may take a little more time than your go-for-broke strategy would if it worked flawlessly, but there is a chance it wouldn't work flawlessly, so you'll come out on top by playing it safe.

This office example illustrates the virtues of small batches:

- Feedback on quality is much quicker and more frequent.
- The risk of waste (in any of the seven categories) is reduced.
- Excess inventory is more easily avoided.

- Customer feedback can be incorporated real time, as opposed to the producer needing to go through inventory before making improvements.
- Level flow is achieved, which often more closely mimics Customer consumption patterns.

The benefit of level flow is especially important when it comes to efficiency.

Do you remember the anecdote about Taiichi Ohno in the supermarket? When he pulled the jug of milk out of its rack, the other jugs lined up behind it slid forward and filled the void just created. This is level flow. Minimal work is done to fulfill the Customer's demand. The product is provided exactly when it is needed, and only then. The most important part of this is the elimination of extra work and, therefore, the elimination of waste.

> "No extra work is done to fulfill the Customer's demand. The product is provided exactly when it is needed, and only then.

A good example of this can be found at your local Subway restaurant. If you pay attention to the setup behind the counter, you'll find that it has been optimized toward a level flow. There are often three team members behind the counter in Subway, and these people typically fulfill the same functions.

- **Person 1:** Determines the kind and size of sandwich being ordered, selects the desired bread type, and places the desired meats on that bread.
- **Person 2:** Places the desired cheeses on the sandwich and asks if the sandwich needs to be toasted; does so if needed. And then, adds any desired vegetables and sauces, and wraps the sandwich in paper.
- **Person 3:** Asks if the Customer wants chips and a drink with their sandwich, puts the sandwich in a bag and rings up the final order.

Have you ever wondered why exactly it is set up in this way? It is to ensure level flow. Each team member's tasks take roughly the same amount of time, and so level flow is achieved. This is why you'll rarely see sandwiches piling up (WIP, or work-in-process) at any stage of the process in Subway. They're always moving through the assembly process at a steady rate due to the level work flow of their creators.

Another, more meta-level example of level flow can be found in the past of one of the giants of American business: Procter & Gamble. One of Procter & Gamble's major areas of production is in household cleaners. In fact, Procter & Gamble invented the idea of "spring cleaning" many years ago as a marketing initiative.

Every spring, they would run a massive marketing campaign for their various cleaning supplies, and demand would go up. In order to meet the high demand, they had huge increases in manufacturing volume, processing, supplying and basically all other areas of the business. But this only happened in the spring, so the volume of work for the rest of the year was always at a steady, much lower level. Their capacity in manufacturing, distribution, and coupon processing needed to surge in one part of the year. They either needed bigger manufacturing lines or needed to fill the surge capacity with contract manufacturers. The same went for warehouses, truck drivers, and many other functions.

Eventually, in the late 1980s, Procter & Gamble realized that its current system just wasn't the best way to do things. They weren't creating a level work flow, and in the chaos of the spring rush each year, the risk of waste and error was very high. In addition, it wasn't at all fair or efficient for the Customer. The idea of spring cleaning was invented, remember? People don't only do cleaning in the spring, they do it all year round. Procter & Gamble was encouraging its Customers to hold excess inventory in their closets. They were following a push strategy rather than a pull strategy: they pushed their products on consumers every spring rather than allowed the consumer to pull products from them. This was inefficient.

So, they decided to de-emphasize the spring cleaning concept and spread production out to fit the Customers' actual demand: lower-level production, all-year round. They achieved level work flow, reducing cost and serving the Customer better.

The Story of the Christmas Ham

We've covered some topics closely connected to the very simple idea of PDCA. But how does a business really begin to implement these ideas? It can often be difficult to affect change in any system, let alone a large organization.

There's an old story about food and Christmas time that might shed some light on this issue. It's the morning of Christmas, and relatives are beginning to arrive at the family home in preparation for the day of merriment ahead. The mother, the hostess of the household, is in the kitchen, focusing on the meal to be served later that night. Her son is watching her work, as she prepares the ham, the centerpiece of any good Christmas feast. He asks his mother how to prepare the ham.

"You wash it, season it, cut off the ends, and put it in the oven to cook. Simple," she says.

"But why do we cut off the ends?" the son asks.

"That's how it's always been done. Why don't you run off now and let me work," Mother replies.

So the son leaves and mingles, but eventually gets curious again and returns to the kitchen.

"Mom, I've been thinking, and I really can't figure out why we cut the ends off the ham."

"That's how it's always been done. Go play with your cousins," Mother replies. This is accompanied by the requisite eye rolls.

After some time, the son returns a third time, and this time, the mother pauses, thinks and then says, "I really don't know. My mother taught me to do it that way."

Later in the day, as the ham lies roasting in the oven, ends cut cleanly off, the kid's grandmother arrives. The son asks her the question of the day.

"Grandma, why did you teach me to cut the ends off the ham before cooking it?" she asks.

"Oh, I don't know," Grandmother replies. "That's just the way my mother taught me."

Later, the great-grandmother arrives. The ham is cooked and ready to be served. The son, his mother, and her mother all greet great-grandmother at the door, and ask, in unison:

"Why do we cut the ends off the ham before cooking it?" Great-grandmother pauses, and then smiles.

"Well, that's easy, I did it because back then my oven was only 12-inches wide. Why do you do it?"

And that is the story of the ham. This is why it is difficult to implement good practices when they aren't already in place — the practices currently in place are already considered good practices and have a momentum, and a constituency of their own. We must question everything in business, and always be looking for a better way to do everything. This is the spirit of PDCA.

There's an old Navy SEALs motto that preaches the same thing: "Always be improving your position."

Related to that exact line, let's talk next about individual goal setting.

Chapter 10

Individual Goal Setting

"Leaders create capacity."

— *Peter Drucker,* The Effective Executive

Earlier in this book, we discussed the importance of setting clear company-wide key imperatives. Companies need goals and targets to shoot for in each quarter and year if they want to have continuing success over time. The same is true for each individual within every company. In this chapter, we dig further and present a system for an individual's personal goals, in the context of one's life inside and outside of work.

In order to be the most successful person you can be — and that definition goes well beyond the one silo of work — you must set holistic, clear key imperatives for yourself. I believe that no amount of success at work can compensate for failure at home. There must be balance, however you characterize it, among the different parts of your life. Whatever your values, having a personal system of goal setting is invaluable. Consistent with the other one-page tools in this book, I have created a one-page personal balanced scorecard to help me allocate energy and resources to achieve my goals.

"Whatever your values, having a personal system of goal setting is invaluable.

Harvard professor Robert Kaplan, originator of the balanced scorecard for business, said that traditional financial goals such as profit or earnings per share, are necessary but not sufficient to measure a company's activity. Earnings are a rearview mirror performance indicator, one that is only evident after all the activity is completed. Kaplan created other categories such as Customer satisfaction and innovation metrics, which have advantages beyond being strictly rearview mirror indicators; they are also more relatable to more people in the company. Asking a line worker in a tech-support call center or a chemist working on the next generation of product what they did today to contribute to EPS may be a confusing question, but asking what they did to advance Customer satisfaction or contribute to innovation may be easier to relate to, and far more motivating for that person.

At the individual level, most of us believe there is more to personal success than making money, and we will be able to relate more closely to when we have goals that reflect those various performance areas. So when you are changing a diaper at 3 a.m., exercising to get in shape, leaving work early for a dinner date with your spouse, or serving others in a charitable function, you'll know what personal KPI is being affected. More important, you can plan for the future, applying your unique values and desires, and create a roadmap and a plan for your precious energy for the next quarter, half-year or year.

The professional goals and objectives (G's and O's) sheet is discussed in detail in Chapter 11. This is a document that can be considered a contract with your company and your manager. This document, along with the personal goals sheet, cover every meaningful aspect of my work life and personal life. Both are equally essential to my success, and I know that I must be diligent in updating both in a timely manner. I personally update and work on the personal goals sheet once per year, and the work goals sheet once per quarter.

PERSONAL GOALS PLANNING

Personal Goals: 20yy

Updated Feb 20yy

Relationships			Health			Career		
Family	Marriage	Network	Physical	Emotional	Religion	Job	Financial	Other Int.
***	***	**	***	**	**	***	***	*
2		*3*		*1*				
• See mom and dad during Summer trip • Have parents over during Thanks-giving • Have spouse's parents over for Christmas	• Continue Imago marriage classes • Have a weekly dinner date with spouse • Have joint personal quiet time without kids 15 minutes per day	• One friends social event per month • Go on NYC weekend trip with friends	• Three runs / week • Three lifts / week • One tennis per week • Stay on Fit for Life nutrition plan • Body fat of 15% (from 17% base) • Focus on abs in gym	• Take girls to school once/ week	• Worship 3 times / month as a family • Do Great Banquet • Volunteer in one Wednesday class as assistant	• 5-S entire office • Complete Six Sigma Black Belt class	• Review wish list monthly • Create and execute charity plan • Hit monthly savings goal	• Read one book a week • Read Atlas Shrugged • 5-S downstairs unfinished room • 5-S walk-in closet

The above picture is an example of a personal goal sheet. As you can see, it is divided first into three main sections: relationships, health and career.

1. **Relationships:** First, we'll look at the relationships section. This is an easy section to pass over. It's easy to pass over not because people don't care about their personal relationships — most people care very much — but rather because most people don't think they can apply performance indicators (or goals) to score their relationships. This simply isn't the case. Obviously, any personal relationship with any single person or group of people is extremely complex, but with a little thought, it is entirely possible and practicable to break it down into actionable goals as a means of improving these relationships overall. Another reason people tend to pass over this section of the goal sheet is because the things listed here, the key indicators of "performance" in your relationships, are what

Stephen Covey would put in his Quadrant II category: They are important, but not urgent; this is in contrast to a deadline or a meeting at work, which are both important *and* urgent. Thus, it is all too easy to neglect personal relationships as they compete for focus with important and urgent demands that occur naturally over time. We often think that personal relationships don't need special tracking or extra focus because immediately urgent matters and life logistics tend to obscure our vision.

This clouding of vision is easily cleared-up. Simply make goals and write them down. Now that we've acknowledged the relationships section of the goal sheet. let's break it down further into three more sections: family, marriage/romantic relationships and network. These sections are fairly self-explanatory.

Under the *family* section, write goals for the next year that are specific and attainable. For example, similar to the image above, you might write that you want to see your parents on summer vacation or have your grandparents (or whatever other family members make sense for you) over for Thanksgiving dinner. Maybe you want to attend more of your daughter's soccer games. These are not complex or overly philosophical or emotional goals. They are simple acts or gestures that lead to opportunities to further strengthen your relationships with your family.

Next is your *marriage or your romantic* relationship, be it with a significant other or with a spouse. Again, it isn't too difficult to think of goals for this category. For example, you might strive to go on a dinner date with your romantic partner once per week, or, if in a marriage with children, you might strive to have joint alone time (no children) per day. Again, these are simple actions that can affect your relationship in a meaningful way.

In the last relationship category is your *network*. This refers to your relationships with friends, acquaintances and colleagues. An example here might be to participate in one friends-only social event per month, or to go on a trip somewhere with friends over Christmas or in the summer. These goals are not as complicated and difficult to boil down as it may seem. Just write them down and do them, and see what happens.

The relationships category is one that is often forgotten for a number of reasons. The next category isn't often forgotten, but is still often neglected.

2. **Health:** It goes without saying that one's health is an eminently important part of one's life. In many ways, one's health *is* one's life. This health isn't limited to the health of one's body, although that kind of health is important. There are two other aspects of one's health measured by the goal sheet that are in many ways just as important as the physical. These are one's emotional and spiritual health areas.

   First, we'll briefly touch on goals for *physical* health. It is especially important in this section to make goals that are measurable and attainable. If you write a goal that says you want to be "super fit" in one year, this goal can be unclear, as "super fit" is not specific enough and can mean almost anything. Instead of a vague proclamation, make goals that are easily broken down and measured. For example, run three times every week, lose 2 pounds per month for 12 months, or bench 200 pounds by July 1. These goals are measurable on a regular basis, which makes them easier to stick with and, in turn, more useful.

   Emotional health is next. This section is one that, like personal relationships, can be difficult to envision in a performance-oriented context. However, it is important to come up with ways to measure emotional health, as it is extremely important in many ways. Obviously, being emotionally healthy is important in itself — life is simply better when this is the case. But having good emotional health also allows you to work hard on other categories of your life, while having poor emotional health might hinder your ability to do so.

It is difficult to give generalized examples of goals for this section. One's emotional well-being and its maintenance is one of the more intensely personal aspects of being human that there is, so it is really up to each individual to think carefully about what makes her emotionally healthy, and then figure out how to break that down into a set of measurable goals. For some, being around their children makes them emotionally healthy. So perhaps a goal might be to drive their children's to school at least once per week. This guarantees them 15-20 minutes with just them, no one else, once per week.

And last under the broader health section is *spiritual* health. In my experience among business people, this category is the one that many people admit they need the most work. Like emotional health, spiritual health is a very personal thing, and it will be completely different from person to person. So again, turning inward and thinking hard about this area of your life can help you come up with goals to measure so that you can improve your spiritual health. As an example, some spiritual goals I've seen included attending services three times per month with their family and to volunteer as a class assistant once per week. But again, just like with emotional health, this section is really up to each individual.

3. **Career:** The last section of the goal sheet is the career section. This is different from the professional goals sheet, which should be updated quarterly and pertain to specific work tasks (more on that later). Like the other major sections of the personal goal sheet, this section is also divided into three smaller sections: job, financial and other interests.

   The *job* section is for your work. Write goals here that will make you better at your job. For example, in the goal sheet image above, one wrote that they wanted to complete a Six Sigma Black Belt class. You might also want to take a class, attend a conference or find a mentor.

The *financial* section takes a little more thought. This section is not necessarily tied to your job, as one's financial success can be defined in a number of ways: accumulating wealth, financing life-long activities (paying for children's education, saving for retirement, paying off house, etc.) and getting out of debt are all examples of possible definitions of financial success, which is why this is a separate category from one's job. Examples of a goal here might be to put a specific amount of money per month into savings, or use a certain amount of money to pay off debt every month.

Last under the career section is *other interests*. This, again, can vary wildly, but it comes down to being simply what one does outside of work that interests them. In his book *You Are the Message*, former White House Press Secretary Roger Ailes writes that a person needs to have read a certain amount of material not pertaining to their job to be what he calls an interesting person. "Who wants to be around someone who can only talk about their job?" he asks. Even the most successful, accomplished individuals have these other interests, even though their jobs are often extremely time consuming and stressful.

Condoleezza Rice is a notable example. She is a perfect model of an well-rounded achiever. As a professor of political science at Stanford University, which is where her professional career began (she served as a professor and provost in the '90s at Stanford), Rice also worked as the National Security Advisor to President George W. Bush during his first term and the Secretary of State for his second. Prior to that, she was part of the National Security Council as an advisor to George H.W. Bush on Soviet and Eastern European affairs. Her career has been diverse, extremely impressive and impactful. And on top of all of that, Condoleezza Rice is a concert-level pianist. This is her other interest.

While we can't all be expected to become expert musicians in our free time, it is healthy to foster and cultivate other interests, if only to simply become a more interesting person. Some examples of goals in this category might be to read one book per week, take a class of some kind or learn to play a certain piece on the guitar. Just something fun and challenging outside of your work life is all you really need here.

That wraps up all the sections of the individual goal sheet. You now know how to fill out each section in order to facilitate personal growth.

Now, let's take steps to analyze and sort goals.

1. **Rating:** On the goal sheet, each subsection has a group of stars (*** like this) in the second row. This is the rating system. When I review the sheet each year, I rate myself on a scale of 1-3 stars (3 being the best) for how well I'm doing in that area.

2. **Ranking:** You'll also see in the example a 1, 2 and 3. These numbers indicate priority ranking. Rank your top three priorities for improvement for the coming time period just underneath the rating area. I choose the top three areas on which I want to really focus my energy and intensity on improving each year.

   Attempting to improve in more than three of the nine areas is asking too much and not prioritizing or focusing my energy, like highlighting every line in a book. One way I choose how to prioritize these areas is by the assigned star rating. As you can see in the example, the person marked the emotional health section with two stars, and also ranked it as priority No. 1 for the following year. However, the person ranked the other interests section with just one star, and yet they have not prioritized that section for improvement. This is because other interests, while important, may not be as urgent or quite as important as other sections on the sheet.

3. **Action Plan:** Without an action plan, goals will just remain goals — they may never be achieved. Develop a plan for each of the nine sections, regardless of rating or ranking. The action plans are simple, easy to review and easy to reconcile with your actual activity. Some can be one-time tasks, such as cleaning the garage or going on a family trip. Others can be regular events, such as going to the gym twice a week, reading 15 minutes a day or mediating every week. I try to have robust action plans for every section, but the high-priority sections have higher intensity goals, reflecting their higher demand of my energy.

Chapter 11

Professional Goals and Objectives

"You cannot be efficient with people"

— *Stephen Covey,* Seven Habits of Highly Effective People

Now that we have our personal goals in order, we can move to the office and sort out the task of establishing professional goals and objectives (G's and O's), with the purpose of achievement in the workplace.

Professional goals are similar to personal goals in that they need to be specific and attainable. However, professional goals are unlike personal goals in that your professional goals may not cast a large net — they are not holistic like your personal goals. No, your professional goals should be focused on only two things: knowing what is expected of you at your job and getting it done.

Who is ultimately responsible for your career? In the previous generation of company men and women, when there was little turnover, and people could expect to spend an entire career with a single company. In that generation it may have been OK to assume the company was responsible for your career and its progression. However, in the current environment, when people switch companies at the rate that the prior generation switched roles within a company, the answer is that you are solely responsible for your career. This cannot be delegated to your company.

"Who is ultimately responsible for your career? You are.

What could be more important than a meeting all about you? That is what the goals and objectives meeting is — a meeting about the direct report in a direct report/manager relationship. This is a regular meeting to:

- Manage your career.
- Get feedback from your manager.
- Express feedback, both positive and negative.

In the indispensable podcast Manager Tools, the hosts say that one-on-one meetings are the single most important management tool there is. If you aren't involved in regular meetings with your direct reports or manager, make launching them a priority.

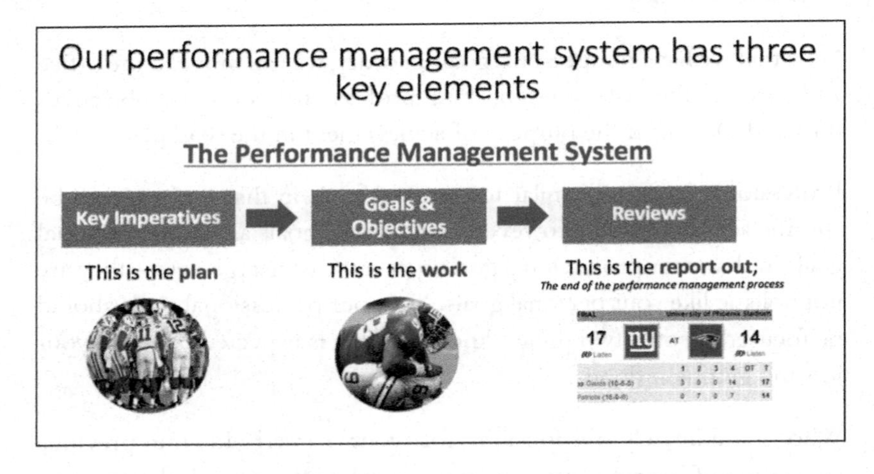

As the diagram above illustrates, key imperatives are the plan to accomplish a goal/objective; goals and objectives are the work it takes to reach them. And the performance review is the end of the performance management process. In this framework, the performance review is a lagging indicator of the work. Like a student that gets nervous opening a report card – the work has already been done, and the performance review is simply documenting the work performed.

Let's describe the core of a performance management system — the work.

In his book titled *First Break All the Rules*, Marcus Buckingham discusses how finding success in a job is like climbing Mount Everest. If you wanted to summit Everest, you would be remiss to think that you could simply fly in a helicopter and step out onto the summit, as if you did so, you would quickly find yourself in dire need of oxygen and suffering from severe altitude sickness. The only safe way to avoid this is to start way down the mountain at base camp, acclimating to the oxygen level at each stage, and working your way up through each camp until you reach the summit.

In this metaphor, Buckingham posits that the base camp of success in a job is best approached by a series of questions, one of which is: Do you know what is expected of you when you show up at work? He says that once you know the answer to this question, and a few others, you can move on to higher altitudes and eventually the summit. But until the answer to the question is "yes," don't climb to the next level–you are not acclimated to your current altitude yet.

The goals and objectives document and the periodic meetings between the direct and the manager have three objectives:

1. **Alignment:** I consider goals and objectives as a contract between the direct and the company. If the direct hits his or her G's and O's, they get a good review; if they don't, they risk getting a poor review. Goals and objectives ensure your work is:
    - What the manager wants you to work on.
    - What the company wants you to work on.
    - What you want to work on.
    - Is not too hard, and not too easy.
    - Documented properly in the goals and objectives document.
    - Aligned for your review.

    Imagine a sailboat leaving the United States and headed toward Europe for a 13-week trip (there are 13 weeks in a quarter). There is a course the boat sets, but over the course of the ocean journey, the boat is subject to tides, winds, navigation error and boat performance. Now imagine the difference in taking a heading adjustment every week, versus once at the end of the quarter. Early and regular course corrections are sure to keep the boat on course, rather than checking in at the end of the trip. Closer alignment means less waste and better performance.

<u>SAMPLE GOALS AND OBJECTIVES SHEET</u>

FOREVER YOUNG CONSULTING

ERIK YOUNG
Goals and Objectives: 1Qyyyy
Updated 2 Dec yyyy, v1.0

= on-track
= some issues
= off-track

Category	Mission	Quarterly Strategy	Goals (SMART)	Due Date	Status
Manage Company Operations	Oversee the operations of the company, ensuring the meeting or exceeding the expectation of our clients	Focus on client touch and listening to the voice of the customer	• Initiate a process to visit clients • Investigate implementing a User Group in 2016	• End of Q1 • End of Q1	
Drive the Scaling-Up of The Company	Implement systems and infrastructure to facilitate the high growth rate of the company and add capacity	Focus on enterprise systems to facilitate company growth	• Coordinate enterprise system to cloud and new system transition plan • Implement Cash Card transition • Drive the business intelligence system to each internal team and expand to clients • Drive the analysis and tool to rate prospect complexity and price accordingly • Begin the transition to a paperless work environment • Drive a tax docket process to manage client tax returns	• End of Q1 • End of Q1 • End of Q1 • End of Q1 • End of Q1 • End of Q1	
Drive Innovation of Systems	Implement systems to further the professionalization of company systems	Support the Leadership Team to implement new systems to improve productivity	• Implement process to reduce WSEs with no email • Support the transition of timeclock operations from AM to Payroll/Onboarding • Drive the transition from old system to new system • Investigate workplace clinic services for company EEs	• End of Q1 • End of Q1 • End of Q1 • End of Q1	
Manage Team of Directors	Manage, coach and develop the Leadership team	Focus on team (department) staff levels, organization, and work expectations transparency	• Manage Directors through G's and O's • Oversee the reorganization of the work teams • Manage the capacity of the organization and implement a process to systematize adding FTEs	• End of Q1 • End of Q1 • End of Q1	
Manage Company Strategy	Support CEO to develop and implement company strategy	Focus on company strategy with regard to growth, business development, and the internal strategy process	• Implement the Quarterly Management Review process • Oversee the company monthly meetings • Create an international PEO partner • Support the company in channel strategy (e.g., verticals, geography)	• End of Q1 • End of Q1 • End of Q1 • End of Q1	
Drive Lean and Continuous Improvement	Use Lean Sigma tools and systems to improve company productivity, increase quality, and reduce waste	Develop a culture of CPAS, RIPS, OPs and structured training	• Publish Phase I of OP manuals (Processing Payroll, Processing Client Taxes, Onboarding 2.0) • Oversee system for one RIP-a-week • Facilitate the training and certification of staff on new OPs • Implement Lean Belt system	• End of Q1 • End of Q1 • End of Q1 • End of Q1	

The above image is an example of a professional goals and objectives sheet (it's one of mine). This sheet shares some similarities with the personal goal sheet, but it is more in depth and all job related. The purpose of this sheet is to allow you a way to ensure that you know the answer to the base camp question: Do you know what is expected of you when you show up to work? I recommend that you update this sheet at least every six months, ideally every quarter.

1. **Category and Mission:** First on the sheet is the "Category" column, and next to that is the "Mission" column. These two columns go hand-in-hand. They are basically an in-depth breakdown of your job description. A one-to-three word title of each job task goes in each row of the category column. A sentence-long summary of each task goes in each row of the corresponding mission column. This part of the table can vary widely from position-to-position and from person-to-person. Typically, people in management positions have personalized

job descriptions, and people in standardized line positions have descriptions shared by everyone in their position. An example of the kinds of things that should appear in these two columns might be:

> *Category: Manage Company Strategy.*
> *Mission: Support the CEO to develop and implement the company direction and long-term plan.*

A meeting with a manager is often essential to validating and getting buy-in to all your responsibilities, and subsequent meetings are often necessary to make sure everything is covered. As these first two columns are the job description, they will need to be updated occasionally, but typically not every quarter like the columns to the right of them.

2. **Quarterly Strategy, SMART Goals and Due Date:** The next rows are "Quarterly Strategy" and "Goals" (SMART ones). The quarterly strategy column describes the strategy related to the category and mission items for the current period. For example, for the category and mission used as an example above, the Quarterly Strategy is:

> *"Focus on company approach to growth, business development, and the internal strategy development process."*

That is the goal for this row for this time period. The goals in the column are deliverables that pertain to the strategy described in the corresponding row of the category, mission and quarterly strategy columns. However, these goals must be what are commonly known as SMART goals. That is, they must be:

- Specific: The goal must address a particular task or process. If while going to the gym you want to get stronger and simply make your goal just that — "get stronger." — it would be a vague goal. You might be a tiny bit stronger after one day at the gym, you may have technically met your goal without achieving anything close to what you intended. It is better to make it your goal to focus on specific input (25 push-ups per day or 25 reps of the bench press) or specific output (bench 200 pounds in one repetition or 180 pounds in five repetitions).

- **M**easurable: The goal must be easily assessed by some metric. This allows its completion to be clear and unambiguous for you and your manager. Examples might be to raise sales by $1 million, complete a training class or publish a report.
- **A**ctionable: The goal must be generally within one's control. For example, if you made it your goal for your large company to achieve a certain price-earnings ratio by the end of the year, that goal would likely not be actionable, as there are a whole lot of factors outside of your control that contribute to a company's price-earnings ratio. (Having a goal of an 80-degree sunny day is unactionable as well.)
- **R**ealistic: the goal must be attainable. Ideally not too easily and not with too much difficulty. To return to the "getting stronger" example, if you have never bench pressed more than 200, and you made it your goal to bench press 250 pounds, you may have set the mark too high. This sounds elementary, but I've seen many CEO's set high goals and miss them consistently.
- **T**imely: the goal must be completed within a specific amount of time. Specify when you are going to hit your goal. With the "get stronger" example, just saying that you want to get stronger is an incomplete goal. Add all of the pieces of SMART together and you might have something like this: "Increase my bench press, squat, and dumbbell curls by 25 percent by the end of the year."

If you put all these components into each goal made in this column, you have a SMART goal. Here's an example from the last row in the template image above: "Publish Phase I of OP manuals (Processing Payroll, Processing Client Taxes,

Onboarding 2.0)." You may notice that this goal doesn't have a time constraint in writing. This is because the time constraints for all goals on this sheet are described in the "Due Date" column adjacent to the "Goals" column. I update my professional goals and objectives sheet every quarter. If the goal is too large to be completed in the quarter, break it down so the smaller goal can be achieved. Oftentimes, early, middle or late in a month is specific enough for a time period.

3. **Status:** In the final column of this table, track your status. Every time you check your goals and objectives sheet (I update mine weekly), you should update the status of each of your goals. For each goal in the "Goals" column, you add a corresponding colored circle.
    - Green signifies that a goal is on track to being completed by its due date.
    - Yellow signifies that there are some issues with the goal.
    - Red signifies major issues.

    This system of visualizing each goal's progress level makes it easy for your manager to review your progress without having to read deeply into each goal. He or she can quickly review the goals marked green and focus only on the yellow and red goals, which of course saves time, but also ensures that those yellow and red circles turn to green circles as quickly as possible.

Using this basic template to manage your professional goals is the best way to ensure that you can pass through base camp on your way up the Everest of job success. You'll be able to describe, at every step of the journey, what exactly is expected of you at work, and you'll be able to cite deadlines, too.

Goals are a key part of any successful person's life. Without setting clear goals, it is easy to lose sight of the things that are important to you and miss good opportunities for personal and professional growth. The two goal sheets we discussed in this chapter are easy to use and will make the process for setting goals and objectives that much easier and that much more effective.

Using the one-page template makes it very easy to communicate your progress with your manager — and, correspondingly, your direct reports' progress with you. I prefer reviewing the "G's and O's" weekly. I have found that the first weekly meetings with people uncover pent-up project management demands and last longer. After a while, a cadence is established, and the manager might just scan the page looking for yellow and red statuses, directing the conversation toward those areas. Ultimately, a lunch meeting may focus for a few minutes on the G's and O's areas that need attention, and the remainder of the time will be spent strategizing or developing a business relationship.

You will find alignment between a direct and a manager is efficient. Alignment is what an army would call a force multiplier.

Can the process of reviewing G's and O's, like any other process, get tedious? Of course it can, and it will. Reggie Miller, the great Indiana Pacers basketball player, made 25,279 free throws in his pro basketball career. He shot 88.8 percent, a very high percentage. He shot 2,560 three-pointers. In an interview with USA Today on Feb. 5, 2011, he said he shot 500-700 shots a day in practice, starting at age 6 and ending when he retired at age 40. I can barely imagine taking 700 shots in one day of my life, never mind every day for over 35 years. Tediousness is discipline. Discipline results in success.

As you progress in your career, you will be more and more accountable for results ("Do") and not effort ("Try"). Perhaps an entry-level cashier at a store can be expected to be unproductive if his cash register software crashes. A CEO reporting bad earnings or cashflow results to a bank is rarely excused by telling the bank they tried really hard. The bank does not care. They require results. It is important for team members, as their careers progress to have tools to help them deliver results.

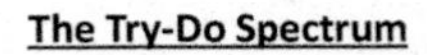

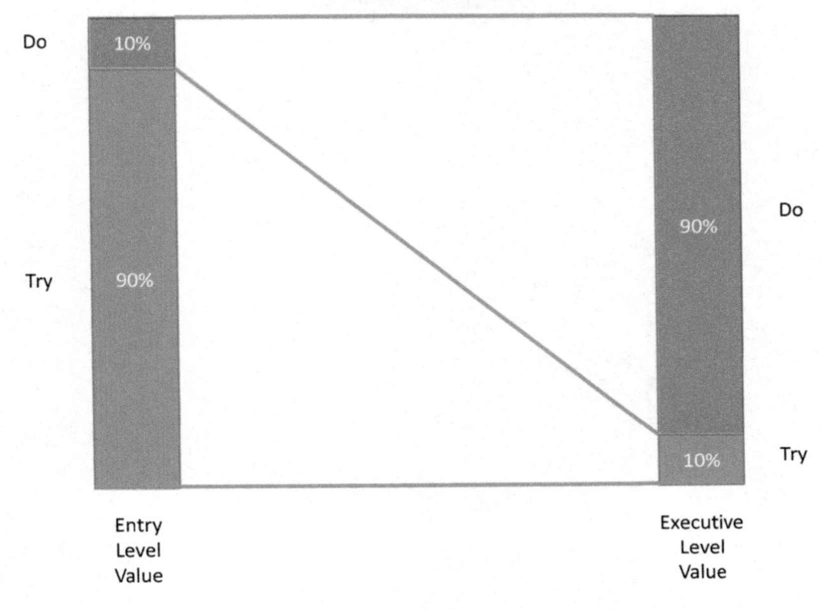

In previous chapters we've discussed concepts of Lean and supporting tools and principles. Next we'll address a make-or-break element of Lean: culture.

Chapter 12

It's not About Tools. It's About Culture.

"Great teams do not hold back with one another. They are unafraid to air their dirty laundry. They admit their mistakes, their weaknesses, and their concerns without fear of reprisal."

— *Patrick Lencioni,* The Five Dysfunctions of a Team: A Leadership Fable

It's Not About the Tools

One of the most counterintuitive but foundational realizations I have had as a Lean operations guy is the realization that it's not about the tools, it's about the culture.

As an avid reader, my goal is to read 24 book a year. There are some books I feel I can read, get the point, and then give the book away. However, there are a handful of books I make a point to reread every few years. They include:

- *The 7 Habits of Highly Effective People*
- *The Five Dysfunctions of a Team*
- *The Purpose Driven Life*
- *Getting Things Done*

Most of these are about the timeless "people aspects" of business and being a social person, rather than mastering a concept or set of business tactics. They stay on the bookshelf; they are part of the permanent collection.

While Lean does have a standard toolkit — the fishbone diagram (see Chapter 8) to find root cause analysis, etc. — it is the cultural aspect of

Lean that is the magical enabler that makes Lean companies great to work in.

Separate the People from the Process

Lean works well in organizations:	Lean doesn't work as well in organizations:
▪ That have buy-in from the top	▪ That are resistant to change
▪ That are open to change	▪ That have fear as a culture
▪ That are transparent	▪ That are "need to know"
▪ That empower team members	▪ That are top-down
▪ Where people are secure	▪ Where people are insecure
▪ Where standard work is good	▪ Where everything is an "art"

I was recently talking to a colleague of mine who has invested in scores of companies and been the attorney for hundreds. He is an adjunct professor at a university teaching entrepreneurship. One of his main messages is that entrepreneurship is not a job description, it is a lifestyle. Relative to getting a job in the corporate world, entrepreneurship may not get you rich, and may even result in a string of short-term high-turnover jobs in your career. But entrepreneurs have a career paradigm of solving the next problem, addressing the vacuum of a product or service, evangelizing to prospects on a product or service they may not realize they need, and having the desire to see the next opportunity just before finishing the last.

I believe being in Lean or continuous improvement is similar — it is a way of life. Lean guys and gals go into a new situation and inherently evaluate and improve. Whether they are at a volunteer charity project, restaurant or beer festival, if they arrive with a Lean mindset, they are mentally leveling the flow, coming up with the critical-to-Customer attributes and reducing waste in their minds.

Lean practitioners are the ones with garages with multicolored floor tape aligned with a laser, and labeled bins. Their food pantries are first-in-first-out to maximize freshness, and their bookshelf is sorted by genre. Their cars get their oil changed on the day their odometer advances by the required 7,500 miles, and the wipers are never old.

Lean guys and gals make order of chaos. If they are not always founding companies themselves, they are supporting the visionaries that create companies. They enable the founders blessed with so much imagination they take wrong turns on the commute to work they have taken for a hundred times. They keep organizations on the right path and resist every shiny object on the road. As a result, they are also the creators.

But in the end they realize there is waste in everything we do, and today's systems are only the current best approach, and the journey is ongoing.

Leadership sets the culture. Procter & Gamble is known for its conservative, analytical culture. If you lost your temper in a meeting, it was an indication of your inability to control yourself and your craft. Conversely, in my first meeting as a consultant at an automobile manufacturing company, I counted the swear words on a piece of paper, losing count at over forty. Managers were much more animated and even yelled. In that company, that was a sign of passion and commitment. Both cultures took after its founders over a hundred years ago, and remained to this day.

The culture of continuous improvement and lifetime learning is critical to seeing Lean succeed in a company. It is far more about how people see friction, conflict and ultimate success as a way of life than mastering technical tools. In evaluating accompany for Lean success, I'll take a positive culture and weak technical skills over the opposite every day of the week and twice on Sunday.

You are a leader, regardless of your title. Lead the culture.

Conclusion

A Springsteen Level of Service

"Learn how to bring it live, and then bring it night after night after night after night. Your audience will remember you. Your ticket is your handshake."

— *Bruce Springsteen*

As we discussed in the previous chapter, it's all about the culture. Culture is the driving force behind any successful company powered by a lean process. It is the glue holding together all the pieces, the stitching holding together all the patches of the quilt. Only a culture healthfully enthusiastic about Lean production will be able to utilize the Lean system to its full potential. There must be a full belief in the system and a full commitment to that belief.

One keystone of a company's culture that drives members to excel, is the concept of service. This is, really, what all businesses do. Service isn't limited to retail stores or restaurants. Service is critical to industries such as manufacturing and health care. In manufacturing, companies strive to diversify the share of revenues generated primarily from product sales to one that includes after-market service and consulting. Every kind of business is doing so. Service, then, is perhaps the only true constant in the business world, and is why companies must prioritize the level of service they provide above all else.

What is the highest level of service? How can it be defined? It is difficult to pin down what good service is in exact terms, but it is one of those experiences where you know it when you see it.

The Best Kind of Boss

A Bruce Springsteen concert is one area where I experience an extremely high level of service. When in high school, my friends and I loved going to concerts. Some popular, big-ticket bands in those days were U2, Billy Joel and "The Boss" himself, Bruce Springsteen. I went to all of these concerts at various points in my youth, but Springsteen's were without question the best deal.

Tickets to U2, Billy Joel and other large, well-known acts usually sold for around $17.50 each. With some variation here and there, the typical concert length for these acts tended to be around 90 minutes — with a considerable delay in starting — and they were great concerts. But Bruce Springsteen exceeded those baseline standards. A ticket to one of his shows was usually about the same price as any of the other high-profile acts of the time, but unlike his fellow big-time rock stars, Springsteen entertained us long into the night. Each concert performed at the Meadowlands from the "Born to Run" tour was four hours long. The Billy Joel and U2 concerts were great, but a Springsteen concert was an ultimate concert experience. I remember heading home from the Meadowlands after midnight - the show started at 8 p.m. sharp. And even though it was late and we'd been on our feet for four straight hours, I always felt the deepest sense of satisfaction after those concerts. I'd truly got what I paid for.

This applies to our world—the business world. Whether as an employee, and CEO, or a consultant, I strive to give a Bruce Springsteen level of service to my Customers. Rather than just doing the minimum level of service for your Customers or partners, and rather than simply doing what is expected of you, strive to give them the equivalent of that four-hour marathon concert instead. Push the boundaries of how much service you can provide, and then go even further. Better yet, don't simply do this a few times for a few Customers, or do this on the most difficult or weighty projects. Become legendary for your level of service every day.

The Boss became The Boss for many reasons, but one of them was certainly his commitment to his audiences. Become The Boss of your industry or your company. Reach the point at which you are sought out by Customers because they have heard stories of your ridiculous commitment to service.

Providing the utmost level of service to Customers and helping other businesspeople do the same through Lean is important to me. It is where I belong.

Frederick Buechner, an American writer and theologian, wrote: "The place God calls you to is the place where your deep gladness and the world's deep hunger meet." In his Venn diagram, the intersection of these two things is something sought after by nearly every person on this planet. I think I've found it.

My first real job was at Procter & Gamble. It was a heavily quantitative and tactical job. I then went to business school, and afterwards Accenture. My job there was on the opposite end of the spectrum—it was mostly qualitative and highly strategic. Once I'd worked both of these jobs, I felt I had a solid background to work in operations in the startup and high-growth company space. It was only through experiencing both sides of the coin that I finally found the intersection of my personal gladness and the world's hunger — Lean operations. I'm truly blessed to have found that place, and that is why I continue to work in this space, and why I decided to write a book like this one — to help businesses provide the highest level of service possible, and maybe, along the way, find their place of gladness and the world's hunger, too.

Thanks for reading.

Select Resources

Chapter 1 US economy

http://www.let.rug.nl/usa/outlines/history-1994/postwar-america/the-postwar-economy-1945-1960.php

Ford Motor Photo

https://en.wikipedia.org/wiki/Ford_River_Rouge_Complex

Japan Manufacturing stats

http://www.nippon.com/en/in-depth/a04003/

Tokyo photo

https://en.wikipedia.org/wiki/Strategic_bombing

Churchill quote

http://www.azquotes.com/quotes/topics/process.html

Nick Saban Quote

http://www.azquotes.com/author/24668-Nick_Saban

Steven Spielberg quote

http://www.mcclatchydc.com/news/nation-world/national/article24718801.html

Henry Ford Quote

http://www.brainyquote.com/quotes/authors/h/henry_ford_2.html"

Einstein Quote

http://www.brainyquote.com/quotes/authors/a/albert_einstein_2.html."

Jordan Quote

http://www.azquotes.com/author/7617-Michael_Jordan

Wooden Quote

http://www.azquotes.com/quote/556580

Deming Photo

https://business901.com/blog1/did-dr-deming-and-peter-drucker-ever-meet/

CPSIA information can be obtained
at www.ICGtesting.com
Printed in the USA
LVOW05s0007081017
551217LV00007B/65/P

9 780692 897041